GOLFLOG

Diary and Guide for the Golfer

Ed Houts
Tim Houts

SPORTSLOG
publishers

Published by Sports Log Publishers, P.O. Box 9275, South Laguna, California, 92677.
Manufactured in the United States.
Cover photograph copyright © 1992 by Gary Newkirk/Allsport. Inside photographs
copyright © 1992 by Sports Log Publishers. Cover and book design by Heidi Sandison,
Laguna Niguel, California.

Books by Sports Log Publishers:
Cycle Log, diary and guide for the cyclist
Golf Log, diary and guide for the golfer
Run Log, diary and guide for the runner
Tri Log, diary and guide for the triathlete and duathlete
Walk Log, diary and guide for the fitness walker

On the cover: Keith Clearwater at the AT&T National Pro-Am 1992 PGA
tournament at Pebble Beach. Clearwater was in the top 15 on the money list
through the U.S. Open in 1992. Photo by Gary Newkirk/Allsport.

Introduction

Welcome to Golf Log.

We at Sports Log Publishers created Golf Log to help you reach your golf goals faster by providing the best diary available to plan and track both your golf rounds and practice sessions. Golf Log features make our diaries the best:

(1) plenty of space to write down all the details of a round or practice session;
(2) concise and helpful tips; and
(3) inspirational photos to keep you motivated throughout the season.

Record your rounds and practice sessions in the diary. Use the tips in the guide to help you reach your goals faster. And enjoy the photos featured throughout the book.

Have a great season of better scores through an improved game.

Good luck!

Ed Houts & Tim Houts

About the authors

Ed Houts
Ed Houts hit his first tee shot at the age of nine on a 135 yard par-3 with a 2-wood. Since then he has improved his game from a 20+ to an 8 handicap through a diligent program of thousands of range balls and hundreds of rounds. Today he builds custom clubs from his Florida shop for a select group of golfers.

Tim Houts
Tim Houts didn't pick up a club until he was 25 and has been hooked on the challenge of improving his game ever since.

Out of his interest in training and competing in all sports, Tim has authored four books on training and racing for triathlon, cycling, fitness walking and running and has studied extensively sports, exercise and nutrition theory.

Acknowledgements
Sports Log Publishers thanks the management and teaching pro staff at Aliso Creek Resort, South Laguna, California for the use of their course in the photographs in this book. Located half way between Los Angeles and San Diego off the Pacific Coast Highway, Aliso Creek Resort offers golfers a challenging course in a picturesque setting.

Table of Contents

PART I: TRAINING GUIDE

PART II: ROUND GRAPHS & TABLES

PART III: TRAINING DIARY

Swing instruction

Four steps will help you lower your scores if you bring a positive attitude and diligence to them: (1) Professional swing instruction, (2) Properly fit, quality equipment, (3) Practice, and (4) Play.

Use swing instruction with Golf Log's training diary to lead you to lower scores by expanding the perspective of "practice makes perfect" into "perfect practice makes perfect." The combination of pertinent drills provided by your teaching pro and a good practice regimen will improve your golfing skill significantly and bring you lower scores, and new levels of enjoyment and appreciation for the game of golf.

Find an instructor that fits you

Take advantage of the instructors available in your area to teach you swing fundamentals and drills to use in your practice sessions and actual rounds.

Almost all golf courses, some practice ranges and many golf stores have instructors available to help you with swing fundamentals and drills. Ask at different locations about the instructors to find one that can help you most.

Good instructors are not necessarily low-handicap or scratch golfers, but are the ones who can best teach and show you the fundamentals and drills. Choose your instructor on the basis of (1) who you feel you can work with and (2) who offers you the level of instruction which can best help your game.

Periodic instruction

Whether you take a series of initial lessons to cover a broad range of swing fundamentals and drills, or if you take periodic sessions to review and solve problem areas, depends on where your game is. But regardless, incorporate regular swing instruction as part of your efforts to improve your game. Because by the nature of the game of golf, all players reach plateaus or hurdles they need help negotiating.

During periodic practice sessions with your instructor, be sure to explain what has been working well and not-so-well with your game. This helps your instructor give you better information and drills to resolve problem areas.

Refer to your notes in your diary regarding specific areas which have improved or degenerated. Work with your instructor as a teammate to improve your game.

Refer to books and videos

Refer to the Other Books and Videos section of this guide for a list of quality books and videos available to help you obtain even more swing instruction. But remember that while books and videos may be very helpful, they can't match the effectiveness of in-person sessions with your teaching pro.

Equipment

Quality golf equipment that fits well is critical to every element of your game and scores. Refer to these sections to research and shop for equipment that is best suited for you.

Clubs

The fit of a set of clubs is important. In an ideal golf world, each player might have their own set of custom clubs fitted to their personal needs. But in the real world, while it is not possible for each player to have a quality set of custom-fitted clubs, there are excellent options available if a good understanding of club fitting is used in their selection.

Club length

When fitting a set of clubs, first determine the club length needed to fit your height and build. Have your local club dealer help you measure the distance between the floor and the tip of your middle finger with your hands hanging comfortably at your side. The average measurement used by manufacturers to develop their standard club length is 27" for men and 26" for women. As a rule of thumb, adjust the club length up or down by 1/4" for each inch greater or less than the average of 27"/26".

Shaft flex

After fitting the club length, find the best shaft flex for your game.

The most important factor in determining shaft flex is your swing speed. Use an inexpensive swing speed measurement tool, such as the Strokemaster, that fits on the end of a club to measure your swing speed, or use your carry distance. This information helps you discuss your needs more clearly with your club dealer:

DRIVER		#5 IRON		
Clubhead Speed (m.p.h.)	Distance of Carry (yds.)	Clubhead Speed (m.p.h.)	Distance of Carry (yds.)	Suggested Flex
Up to 52	Up to 135	Up to 40	Up to 89	Very Flexible
53 to 67	136 to 170	41 to 54	90 to 115	Flexible
68 to 82	171 to 210	55 to 68	116 to 145	Regular
83 to 97	211 to 245	69 to 82	146 to 175	Stiff
98 and up	246 and up	83 and up	176 and up	Extra Stiff

Club lie

Clubs come in standard, flat and upright lies. These different lies allow for variables in an individual's height, arm-to-ground distance and ball-address position.

Be sure your club lie fits you. The club sole should rest evenly on the ground at ball address. Neither the toe or heal of the iron should be elevated.

Club heads

There are three types of stainless steel widely used in the golf club investment casting process today. They are from hardest to softest: 17-4, 431, and 18-8 (or 304). A harder head will yield longer distances, but less feel. Choose a head that matches your game.

Grips

Grips that are too large can inhibit your wrists during the swing causing a slice. Grips that are too small can encourage your wrists to work too much, causing a hook. Standard grip sizes tend to be a little too small for most golfers today. Ask your club dealer to be sure to fit the grip to your hands.

Balls

There are two major categories of balls: (1) 2-piece and (2) 3-piece. Traditionally, 2-piece balls are made with synthetic covers, yield longer distance, cost less, and are more durable but offer less feel and spin ability. Conversely, 3-piece balls traditionally are made with soft covers which give good feel and spin ability, but are less durable, give less distance and cost more. Choose balls on your needs.

Shoes

Look for three things in a shoe: (1) comfort, (2) performance, and (3) style. Use your larger foot to establish size. There should be at least 1/4" of space between your big toe and the toe of the shoe. Be sure the fit across the ball of your foot is secure but not tight, and check that there is no play in the heel when you walk. Lace the shoes. If the eyelets on either side touch, the shoe is too big.

Be sure the shoes offer adequate support through the arch and that the spikes give good traction on wet grass.

Glove

Use of a glove is a personal preference. A glove can offer improved grip for many players, but may not provide adequate feel for others. Try a glove to see if it helps your swing and game.

In fitting a glove, be sure your fingers flex easily. The leather should be raised slightly away from your palm when your hand is outstretched. Look to see that the material fits flush against the skin at the base of each finger.

Pants and shirt

Observe the saying in the industry that if a pair of pants or a shirt are too big, they fit. Keep in mind that your waist expands two inches when you sit or squat, and you'll be doing a lot of that on the golf course.

Rain/wind jacket

Freedom of movement is the key. Before purchase, try on the jacket and take some practice swings. If there is tightness in the back or binding in the left shoulder, get the next larger size.

Get more from your game

Improvements in your game can come from many areas. Use the following tips to help you get more from your game:

Set Goals
As with any successful endeavor, the usual buzz-words of "dedication," "hard work," and "perseverance" apply to improving your golf game. Obviously, implementing a good practice ethic for only three or four sessions will not enhance your game permanently.

Set realistic short and long term goals.

For example, suppose your handicap is a 20. Your long term goal might be to lower your handicap to a 16. Short term goals to help reach this larger goal might be: (1) 2 instructor sessions per month, (2) 1 practice session per week, (3) 3-4 actual rounds per month, and a reduction from 45 putts per 18 holes to 36-38 putts per 18.

Track your handicap
If you're not part of a handicapping program, we urge you to join one. It's simple and inexpensive.

Ask your local golf shop. Many have software to track your handicap and the cost is usually no more than $30.00 per year. Your handicap is a direct reflection of your level of expertise, and it provides a good yardstick to measure improvement.

Save your score cards and date them. Record here in Golf Log your scores, dates, course slope, and course rating as the important information used in figuring your handicap. Plan on a minimum of ten scores to establish a fairly firm handicap.

While an average score of several rounds does not take into account the more complex variables a handicap does, your average score is still a useful indicator of your game.

Use the Average Score chart in this guide to figure and track your average score.

Play tournaments to improve your game
As long as golf continues its popularity, there will be many organized competitive tournaments available with a variety of formats. Participate!

Nothing builds confidence quicker than being able to deliver under pressure. And tournaments give you this experience.

Play your lie and putt out

Another simple but often overlooked way to improve your game during actual rounds is to play the ball where it lies. Unless prevailing rules allow relief, playing your lie forces you to play through adversity. This gives your game and confidence a big boost.

On the putting green, don't concede short putts to yourself. Play the ball 'til it rattles the bottom of the cup!

Play two balls

Play two balls while playing a round during the evening or on a slow day. Play best ball, or play each ball through the entire round to give you more practice and lies from different places on the course. Be sure to play each ball with purpose and concentration or this drill will be less effective.

Basic practice session

In arranging practice sessions to get more out of your game, these suggestions will maximize your efforts:

Find a good practice range

Not all practice ranges are created equal. Choose the best range available to you in your area to help you get the most out of your practice session time.

Early in your season it may be enough to use a range with marked distances only; but as you progress through the season and your game improves, a range's specific features become more important.

Use these criteria to select a good practice facility:

1. Good quality balls
2. Grass to hit off
3. Sand-trap
4. Putting green
5. Pitching green
6. Measured green areas with accurate distances to aid club selection.

Structure your practice sessions

Ideally, practice time should be reasonably open-ended. Give yourself plenty of time to have a quality, focused practice session without being rushed.

Hitting a quick bucket of balls during lunch is not a good approach. Odds are that you'll hit some bad shots and come away wondering what went wrong. Further, a hurried session will not generate good muscle-memory or a reliable "swing-key."

Stretch

Stretch and loosen up prior to a practice session or an actual round. Combine these stretches with your pre-practice session and pre-round routine to prevent injury or pulled muscles and to give you better scores.

Lower back & leg stretch

To stretch your lower back (and your hamstrings additionally), stand with your feet together and your knees straight. Slowly bend at the waist and try to touch your nose to your knees and your hands to your toes. Hold for 30 seconds.

Upper body & lower back stretch

While standing, pull your right hand from over your head toward the left side of your body. Let your upper body bend to the left. Feel your shoulder and side of your rib cage stretch.

Repeat with left hand and other side of upper body.

To further stretch and warm up your back and chest area, while standing, twist you torso first 90 degrees to the left then 90 degrees to the right. Twist slowly and easily to stretch safely. Repeat several times.

Ease into your practice session
After stretching, ease into practice session by first hitting 8-12 balls with a 9-iron. Swing easy during this warm up. Concentrate on feel and loosening up more than distance or accuracy.

Then hit another 8-10 balls with a middle iron.

Finally, hit 4-6 balls with your driver. Now you should be loosened up and ready for a practice session.

Use this same warm up routine before you play an actual round to loosen up as well as to alert your body that it is time to play some good golf.

Pre-swing routine
Before each swing, take one or two practice swings at a specific target on the ground and see the shot in your mind.

Think through the practice swing.

Develop a pre-swing routine that you take on the course with you. Do the same pre-swing routine in the practice session just as you would on an actual round.

Set up drill
During your first set of balls, pick a target and lay two clubs parallel and about 2 1/2 feet apart aimed at the target. Lay a third club at an angle on the club farthest from your stance. The angle should simulate the inside-out path of your swing.

Tee the ball between the parallel clubs and stand square to them. Concentrate on your swing plane during this early part of your practice session. The ball direction will be lined up by the parallel clubs. Use the angled club as a visual reminder of the inside-out path your club should travel. Use this aid until you're warmed up and ready to pick specific targets and play particular shots.

Build muscle memory with swing keys
Muscle memory is what you build with every swing you take in practice. It is what you take onto the course with you each round. And "swing keys" help you trigger your correct muscle memory for your best swing.

During each swing of your practice session, develop certain "keys" that trigger a "go/no-go" feeling. Look and feel for certain "Swing Keys" which help keep your swing in the groove. The forward press is one key to start the swing. Another key during take-a-way is to feel right elbow pressure on your rib cage until body rotation moves your elbow away from your body.

Whatever keys you develop, maintain your tempo so it does not exceed your ability to count off the keys during the swing. This is especially true during practice sessions. Eventually, the swing keys will trigger your muscle memory and your body will execute your ideal swing without thinking during your round.

Additionally, these swing keys you develop are good analytical tools that will help you find your groove again after the occasional times your swing falters. And that happens to all of us now and then.

Tempo drill

Timing and tempo is essential to a good swing. Use this drill to work on building the correct tempo of your swing into your muscle memory:

Count off "1," "2," "wait," "3" during your swing. Count "one" as you begin to swing back. Count "two" as you come further back on your swing. Say "wait" at the top of your swing. Count "three" as you begin to swing your club down. Adjust how quickly you count through this "1, 2, wait, 3" on your own swing tempo.

Work through your clubs

Start with a wedge if your practice session is to include work with all your clubs.

Work diligently with just your 8-iron if you don't have to time to work with all of your clubs during your practice session.

Use this routine as a starting structure for your practice session. Develop your own routine as you get a feel for what works best for you.

(1) Make some preliminary swings to simply feel the club and let it become an extension of your arms. Vary the swings through partial to full.

(2) Pick out a target 15 or 20 yards away and adjust your swing speed to hit the target. Be sure to swing through the ball—no stopping allowed.

(3) Increase target distance until you reach a comfortable maximum—no overswinging. Keep reminding yourself of rhythmic tempo. Be patient. According to Jack Nicklaus, he seldom swings more than 85% of max.

(4) Repeat this routine with each club. Your log pages provide adequate space to jot down results. Don't depend on memory alone to recall problem areas. If, for example, you hit a majority of balls to the left, note it.

Learn from other clubs

Hit with a different club to cure some problems (for example, hitting to the left) which may come up during a practice session. Then go back to the problem club and see if the problem is still there. This information generates a good basis for your learning process and will help your instructor zero in on problem areas.

As you move from one club to the next, record the minimum information outlined on the practice diary pages. Note especially (1) distance and (2) direction with each club. Don't become a "golf ball machine gun." Hit each ball with purpose and patience. The session may seem slow; but remember, your reasonably-paced round at the golf course takes about 4 hours.

Note average distances

As you accumulate data on each club, a pattern will emerge. Come to think automatically of a specific club for a specific distance.

Club distance varies from one individual to the next. While an 8-iron may be a 150 yard club for some, it may be 120-125 yards for others. Specific clubs and specific distances are not arbitrary. Note your distance average for each club in the log.

From time to time, you will hit the ball farther than usual. It's that magical moment when all moving parts work in total harmony.

Don't use that yardage as your goal distance for that club. This will erode rhythmic tempo until you are swinging out of your shoes on every shot.

Over-club slightly

Don't be embarrassed to pull out a 3, 4, or 5 wood to cover a 200 yard distance after your partner just covered the same yardage with a 4-iron.

Over-club slightly to promote a more relaxed swing and increase your confidence to negotiate the distance.

Fight the urge lurking in each of us to "crush" every shot, especially the drive, and then saunter off the tee to oohs, aahs, and accolades of your group. A medium distance shot on to the sweet spot of the fairway will lead to oohs and aahs over your scorecard in the clubhouse, while a "crushed" shot out-of-bounds will lead to a ball hunt in the woods.

Imaginary hole drill

Use this drill too finish out this part of your practice session:

At the range, play an imaginary hole at your local course: Visualize your favorite hole. Tee up the ball for your drive. Set up and swing. Note the location of your drive and imagine where it would be on the course hole. Select the next club and continue your approach until you are on the green and ready to putt.

Extend this drill to include some of the holes that give you the most trouble. With this technique you can replay the hole until you develop a valid attacking strategy.

Short game

The leader in greens-hit-in-regulation on the PGA Tour seldom exceeds 75%. This means that even the best player in this category has to negotiate 25% of his holes with a reliable short game. A precision approach and a one-putt par can make up for that missed shot between tee and green.

Learn to hit aggressively
The short shot pitched over a bunker is the most important stroke-saving shot in the game outside of a long putt. Learn to play the shot aggressively onto the green to avoid hitting timidly into the sand and adding wasted strokes onto your card.

Remember tempo
Play short pitch and other precision shots carefully and with added focus. Use the "1,2, wait, 3" drill to help you get rhythm into the shot. Take more of a backswing than you think you need.

Up & down drill
Use the following drill to develop your short shot confidence and ability:

Use your backyard or a nearby field for this drill. Use an old piece of carpet to hit off and an old tire or any other stationary object as a target. Vary the distance from 10 to 50 feet away from the target. Hit the ball and loft it softly into the tire. Don't be satisfied with the ball bouncing onto the target. Hit the target softly on the fly.

Then during your actual round, study the green carefully and select a landing area that will allow your ball to get up to or past the pin. Remember, never up, never in.

Practice with and use the club you have the most confidence in for these short precision shots.

Obstacle drill
Incorporate an obstacle as an extension of the Up & Down Drill to simulate hitting over a sand trap or other obstacle on your way to the green. Use a fence, small pond, small tree, or range sand trap for an obstacle. As in the Up & Down Drill, vary the distance from the target, but concentrate on feeling confident as you stroke the ball. And remember, as in the other drill, don't be satisfied with the ball bouncing onto the target. Hit the target softly on the fly.

Create your own shot scenarios.

Sand trap drill
Develop solid swing ability in your other clubs before practicing your sand trap shots. Remember that most short sand shots require an outside-in, vertical swing

path. Hit the sand an inch or so behind the ball and accelerate through it. The ball floats up on a cushion of sand and the club head never actually touches the ball.

Build your sand trap ability and confidence with this drill:

Work from three locations in a green-side sand trap: (1) the up-slope near the bunker lip closest to the green, (2) the flat part in the middle of the trap, and (3) the down-slope of the trap away from the green.

Hit 10-12 balls from each location in the bunker. Regardless of results, develop a positive attitude toward your bunker shots. With continued practice and some key instruction you will develop confidence and success in your bunker shots.

Putting

According to expert golf analysts, putting is 43% of the average golfer's score. In this perspective, putting obviously must become an important part of your practice time. (And your putter certainly needs to be properly fitted.)

Work on short and long putts
The four-foot putt has been rated by many pros as one of the toughest shots in golf. Spend as much time on this putt as on the 10-15 foot putts or closer.

Start and finish practice sessions with putting
Start practice sessions with 10-15 minutes of putting and then close out the session with another 8-10 minutes. Invent games on the practice green, especially trying to two-putt from outside of 15 feet.

Concentrate on each putt
From long range, aim for an imaginary 6-foot circle around the pin. You'll be surprised how often some of these will drop. During the putting session, be sure to have purpose in each putt. Read the green and establish your own ritual before actually stroking the ball. Avoid standing over the ball until your knuckles turn white. Stroke with decisive confidence.

Putt from all lies
Practice from various locations on the green and include balls resting on the first cut and even balls up against the fluff of the second cut. You may not putt these different lies often, but the shots will become viable options during rounds if you have practiced them.

Make each putt twice
Whether on the course or on the practice green, always make each putt twice: (1) Visualize the putt. See yourself striking the ball. See the ball roll along the line. And see it drop in the hole. (2) Transfer the mental picture into an actual putt.

Grip drill
A good grip is the basic factor in all good golf. This is true of all strokes, but especially true of the putting stroke. The grip should be firm but comfortable.

Concentrate on keeping a firm grip with the little finger of your left hand (for right-handed players). This will help your middle two fingers keep a firm grip, which will help your putting stroke. Ask your swing instructor to help you refine your finger position and pressure. Remember to stroke the ball firmly. Don't baby it.

Try the following drill to build muscle memory into your grip:

Find a discarded club with a reasonable grip on it, or have your local pro make a club grip for you. Keep the grip in the car, at home or at work with you. Periodically, pick up the grip and work with it for 1-2 minutes at a time. Check your grip for proper position and feel.

String drill

It is critical to follow through your putting stroke squarely to prevent pushing or pulling your putt. Use a properly fitted putter to help prevent pushing or pulling. And use this drill to work on your putting follow-through stroke:

Tie a piece of string to the pin on the practice green. Stretch the string 4-10 feet from the pin. Tie the other end of the string to a piece of coat hanger; insert the coat hanger into the ground so the string is 4 inches above the ground.

Place the ball squarely under the string and practice your stroke. Check to see that your stroke and follow-through is on-center and square.

4-ball drill

Use this drill to build putting tempo and ability:

Place four balls around the cup at 12, 3, 6 and 9 o'clock positions about 2 feet from the hole. Putt each one in. If you miss one, start over. After making all four, move the four balls out to a 3-foot circle and putt each in. Be sure to start over if you miss a putt. Repeat these four ball circles at the 4, 5 and 6 foot circles.

Hard/Easy drill

This drill will give you further help on your putting and can also be used as a warm-up drill prior to an actual round:

Hit three balls toward the hole. Hit the first ball obviously too weak. Hit the second ball obviously too hard. And hit the third ball in between the first two. This will give you a feel for the greens and your stroke.

Other books & videos

Golf Log's training guide offers tips and drills to help you get more out of your game. Refer to these books and videos for more in-depth discussions of other golf topics:

Books
Gallwey, Timothy: The Inner Game of Golf, Random House
Hogan, Ben: The Modern Fundamentals of Golf, Fireside Books/Simon & Schuster
McLean, Jim: Golf Digest's Book of Drills, Pocket Books
Nicklaus, Jack: Jack Nicklaus' Lesson Tee, Fireside Books/Simon & Schuster
Ostroske, W. & Devaney, J.: Two-Putt Greens in 18 Days, Perigee Books/Putnam
Toski, B. & Fleck, J.: Find Your Own Fundamentals, Pocket Books
Watson, Tom: Tom Watson's Getting Back to Basics, Pocket Books

Videos
Armstrong, Wally: Maximizing Your Game & Everything About It, Gator Golf, Maitland, FL
Armstrong, Wally: Golf for Kids of All Ages, Gator Golf, Maitland, FL
Armstrong, Wally: Pictures Worth A Thousand Words, Gator Golf, Maitland, FL
Armstrong, Wally: Golf, Gadgets and Gimmicks, Gator Golf, Maitland, FL
Armstrong, Wally: Feel Your Way to Better Golf, Gator Golf, Maitland, FL
Miller, Johnny: Golf the Miller Way, Morris Video, Torrance, CA
Rosburg, Bob: Bob Rosburg's Break 90 in 21 days, Simitar Entertainment, Plymouth, MN

How to get more from your diary

The purpose of Golf Log is to help you develop the most effective practice routine based on notes of your actual rounds.

Use the Golf Log Practice and Play diary pages to keep track of your practice drills and your successes and problems on the course. And use Golf Log to help keep you honest and focused to your goals of improving your game.

Record streaks on Play pages

Be sure to note periods of exceptional play. These streaks may last for 2 or 3 holes, 2 or 3 shots, or 2 or 3 rounds. Take notice and record what is working well and why. For example, you may realize that your level of concentration is better than usual or your iron shots are especially crisp and accurate. Use this information during other periods to find your best golf again.

Transfer key information from your scorecard

Take time to transfer key information from your scorecard while the round is still fresh in your mind. Be sure to note: birdies, pars, bogeys, double bogeys, greens in regulation, total putts, and fairways hit.

Try the following abbreviations on the course for scorecard notes: Mark Fairway (H)it, (L)eft or (R)ight in the upper left corner of each hole's box; mark Green in (REG)ulation in the upper right; record number of putts in lower right, and; note (B)irdie, (P)ar, (BO)gey in the lower left.

Also be sure to note any problem areas that may come up which need special attention in your next practice session.

Use the graphs included to track your progress in: total score, number of putts, greens in regulation, fairways hit, and birdies.

Note average distances on Practice pages

As you accumulate data on each club, a pattern will emerge. Come to think automatically of a specific club for a specific distance.

Club distance varies from one individual to the next. While an 8-iron may be a 150 yard club for some, it may be 120-125 yards for others. Specific clubs and specific distances are not arbitrary. Note your distance average for each club in the log.

From time to time, you will hit the ball farther than usual. It's that magical moment when all moving parts work in total harmony.

Don't use that yardage as your goal distance for that club. This will erode rhythmic tempo until you are over-swinging on every shot.

SCORE AVERAGE

ROUND NO/DATE	ROUND SCORE	CUMULATIVE TOTAL	AVERAGE (CUM.÷ ROUND #)
1 3/3/94	41	41	41
2 3/4/94	37	78	39
3 3/11/94	42	120	40.
4 3/12/94	47	167	41.8
5 3/18/94	46	213	42.8
6 3/25/94	40	253	42.2
7 4/1/94	43	296	42.3
8 4/2/94	42	338	42.3
9 4/9/94	43	381	42.3
10 4/16/94	44	425	42.4
11 4/19/94	39	464	42.2
12 4/29/94	40	504	42.0
13 4/30/94	43	547	42.1
14 5/20/94	39	586	41.9
15 6/27/94	43	629	41.9
16 7/8/94	36	665	41.6
17 7/14/94	46	711	41.8
18 7/29/94	44	755	
19			
20			
21			
22			
23			
24			
25			
26			
27			
28			

SCORE AVERAGE

ROUND NO/DATE	ROUND SCORE	CUMULATIVE TOTAL	AVERAGE (CUM.÷ ROUND #)
29			
30			
31			
32			
33			
34			
35			
36			
37			
38			
39			
40			
41			
42			
43			
44			
45			
46			
47			
48			
49			
50			
51			
52			
53			
54			
55			
56			

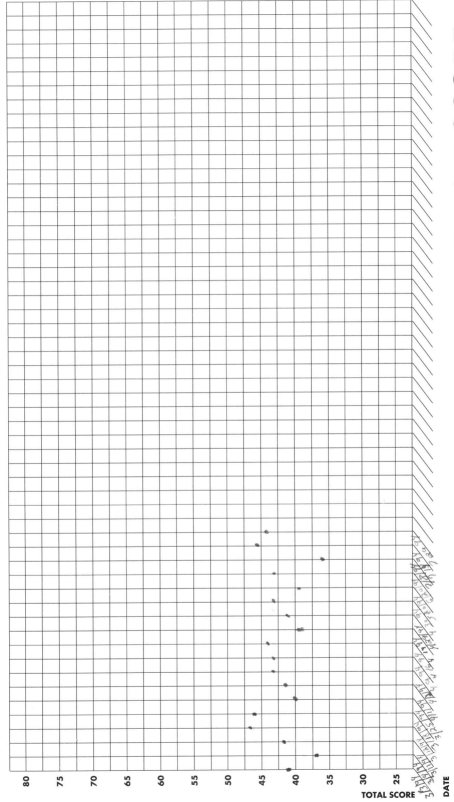

9 HOLE **SCORE**

TOTAL SCORE

DATE

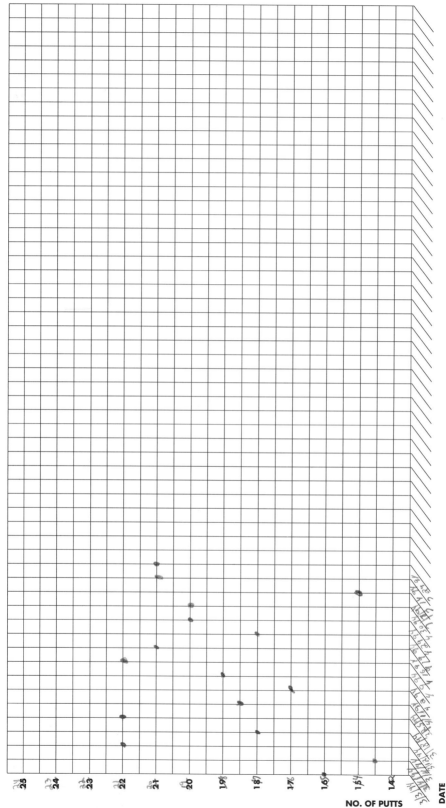

9 HOLE **PUTTS**

25
24
23
22
21
20
19
18
17
16
15
14

NO. OF PUTTS

DATE

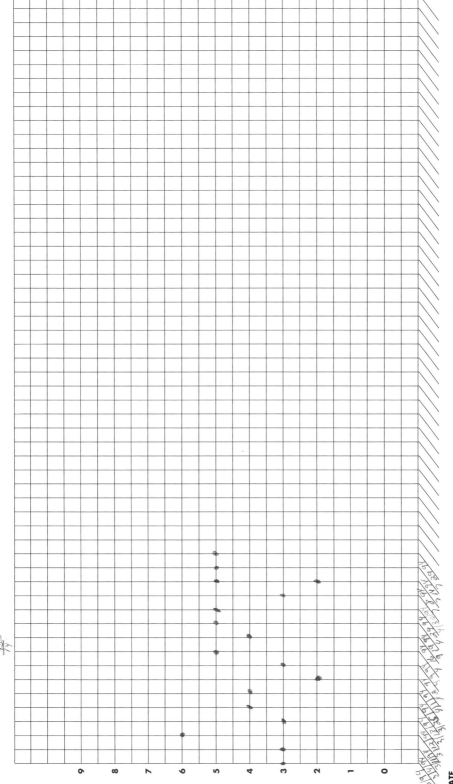

9 HOLE **GREENS**

NO. OF GREENS REACHED IN REGULATION

DATE

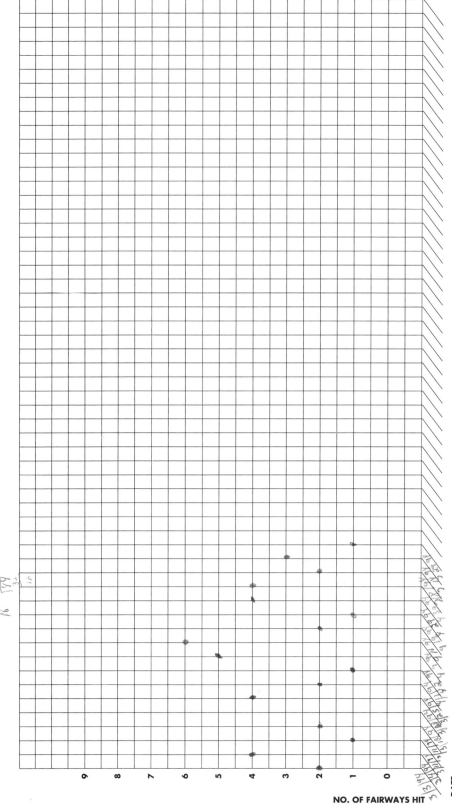

9 HOLE **FAIRWAYS**

NO. OF FAIRWAYS HIT

DATE

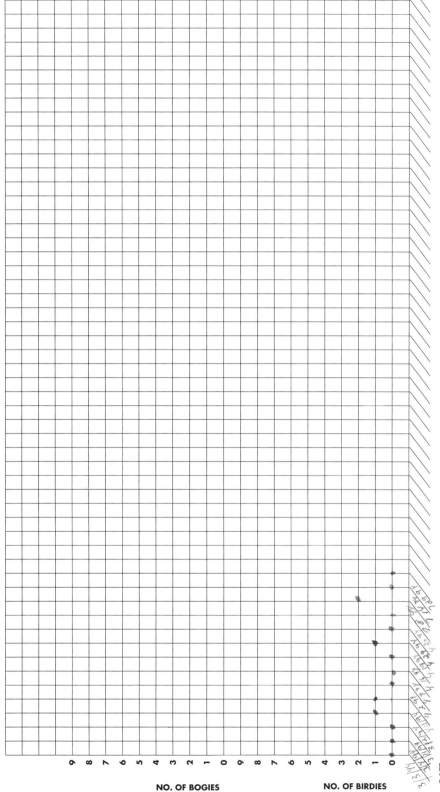

9 HOLE **BIRDIES**

NO. OF BOGIES

NO. OF BIRDIES

DATE

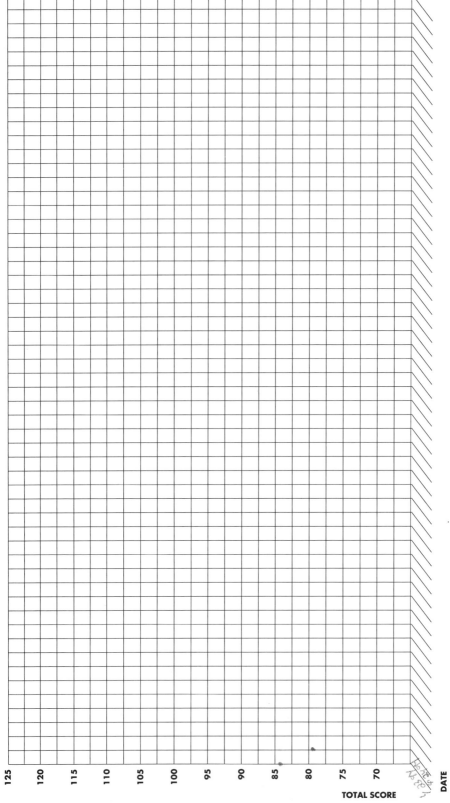

18 HOLE **SCORE**

125
120
115
110
105
100
95
90
85
80
75
70

TOTAL SCORE

DATE

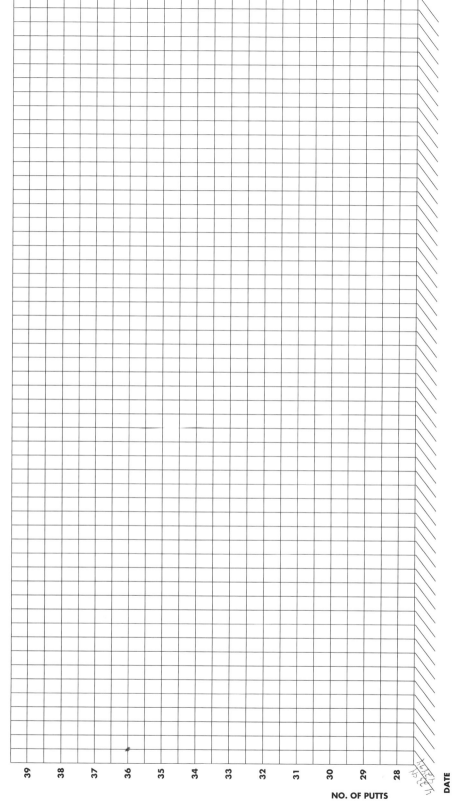

39

38

37

36

35

34

33

32

31

30

29

28

NO. OF PUTTS

DATE

18 HOLE PUTTS

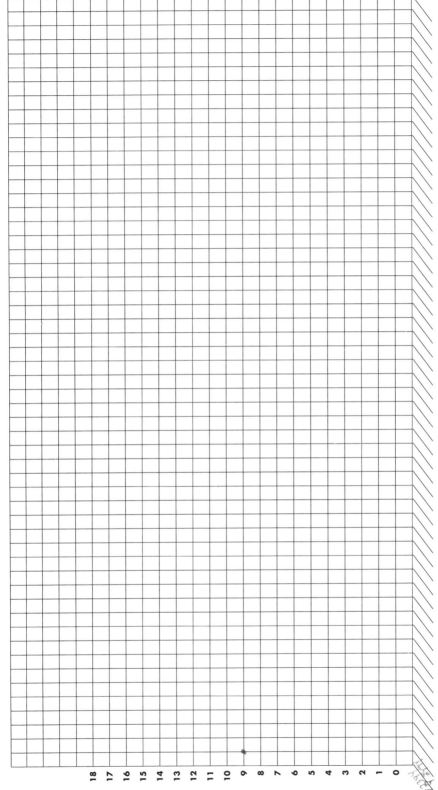

18 HOLE **GREENS**

18
17
16
15
14
13
12
11
10
9
8
7
6
5
4
3
2
1
0

NO. OF GREENS REACHED IN REGULATION

DATE

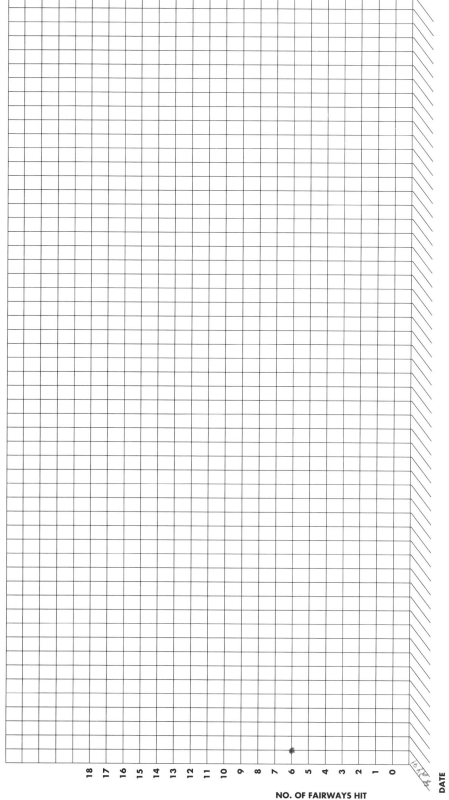

18 HOLE **FAIRWAYS**

18
17
16
15
14
13
12
11
10
9
8
7
6
5
4
3
2
1
0

NO. OF FAIRWAYS HIT

DATE

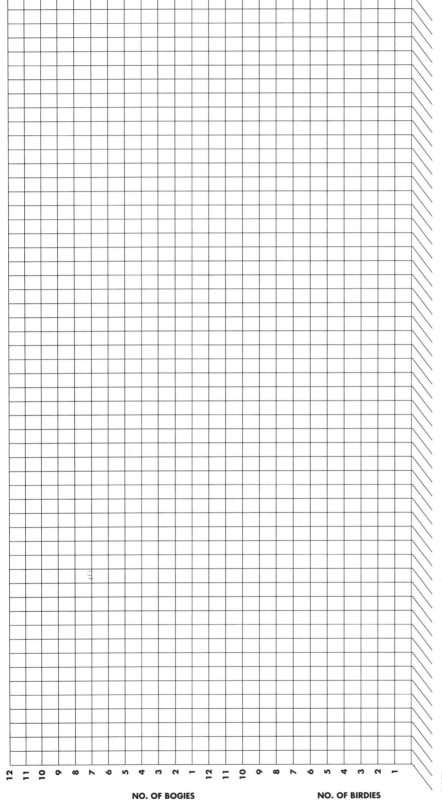

18 HOLE **BIRDIES**

12 11 10 9 8 7 6 5 4 3 2 1 12 11 10 9 8 7 6 5 4 3 2 1

NO. OF BOGIES **NO. OF BIRDIES**

DATE

"There's no such thing as natural touch. Touch is something you create by hitting millions of golf balls."

-Lee Trevino

PLAY

COURSE Valley Oak, Visalia CA

	TEE SHOT-HIT FAIRWAY(F), OR MISSED LEFT (L), RIGHT (R)	GREEN IN REGULATION (G), MISSED LEFT (L), MISSED RIGHT (R)	up/down/# OF PUTTS / SCORE / PAR

OUT

1			
2			
3			
4			
5			
6			
7			
8			
9			

SCORE

IN

10	R, slice, playable / Driver	G, Hit approach into cup / 5 iron	10 / 2 / 4
11	R, slice, trees / 2 iron ("played "safe")	Hit tree, 3rd 12 ft from pin / 6 iron, Hit thin	11 / 4 / 4
12	F, slice / Driver	L, slice, trees / 3 iron	N / 2 / 6 / 5
13	F, slice / Driver	L, stubbed iron / PW	Y / 1 / 5 / 5
14	Par 3	G, fade / 7 iron	3 / 4 / 3
15	F, skyed / Driver	R, push slice / 5 wood	N / 2 / 5 / 4
16	R, slice, water / Driver	3rd shot G / 8 iron	1 / 2 / 4 / 4
17	L, pulled / 3 iron	Pitch was short 10 ft / SW	N / 2 / 4 / 3
18	R, slice / Driver	L, Pull hook / 4 iron	N / 2 / 5 / 4

BIRDIES	0	# GREENS IN		NOTES FOR NEXT PRACTICE SESSION: Straighten	41
PARS	2	REGULATION	3	slice, stop stubbing	**SCORE**
BOGEYS	5	# PUTTS	15	short irons. Slow tempo	41
DOUBLE BOGEYS	1	# TEE SHOTS HIT	2	down.	**TOTAL SCORE**

PLAY

COURSE Ancil Hoffman, Sacramento CA

	TEE SHOT-HIT FAIRWAY(F), OR MISSED LEFT (L), RIGHT (R)	GREEN IN REGULATION (G), MISSED LEFT (L), MISSED RIGHT (R)	up/down	# OF PUTTS / SCORE / PAR
OUT				
1	R, Slice, Trees	L, short	Y	1 / 4 / 4
	Driver	8 iron	Pitch SW 6ft	
2	R, Slice, Trees	short	Y	1 / 5 / 5
	Driver	3 iron 200y	chip SI 8ft	
3	L, Push Slice, Trees	G	NA	2 / 4 / 4
	Driver	9 I	15ft	
4	F	R, Push, Sand	Y	1 / 4 / 4
	3 I	7 I soft	SW 3ft	
5	4ft from cup	G	NA	2 / 3 / 3
	5 I			
6	F, gentle fade	L, pulled, sand	Y	1 / 4 / 4
	D	5 I	SW 4ft	
7	F, straight	G (Topped 3W on 2nd shot)	NA	2 / 5 / 5
	D	5 I	15ft	
8	F, gentle fade	L, Pulled, sand	N	2 / 5 / 4
	D	8 I	SW 6ft	
9	R, Push fade, sand	No	Y	1 / 3 / 3
	5 I		SW & 1ft	**37**
				SCORE

IN

10				
11				
12				
13				
14				
15				
16				
17				
18				

37
SCORE

BIRDIES 0	# GREENS IN	NOTES FOR NEXT PRACTICE SESSION: FW woods.
PARS 8	REGULATION 3	Approach shot with irons.
BOGEYS 1	# PUTTS 13	
DOUBLE BOGEYS 0	# TEE SHOTS HIT 4	

TOTAL SCORE

PLAY

DATE 3/11/94
DAY Friday
RATING/SLOPE 90.9 / 119

COURSE Valley Oak, Visalia CA

	TEE SHOT-HIT FAIRWAY(F), OR MISSED LEFT (L), RIGHT (R)	GREEN IN REGULATION (G), MISSED LEFT (L), MISSED RIGHT (R)	up/down	# OF PUTTS / SCORE / PAR
OUT				
1	R, Slice	G Slightly Pushed		2 / 5 / 5
	3 I	PW		
2	R, Slice	G		2 / 4 / 4
	Driver	5 I soft		
3	R, Fade	G fringe		3 / 5 / 4
	Driver	8 iron	40 ft	
4	F, Gentle Fade	G		3 / 5 / 4
	Driver	?	35 ft	
5	R	G Push		2 / 3 / 3
	6 I	6 I 168yd w wind	35 ft	
6	R, Slice sand	5 sand	N	3 / 6 / 4
	Driver	9 I	15 ft short	
7	L, Pull, sand		N	2 / 4 / 3
	3 I 205		4 ft	
8	L, Bad Pull	Escape shot under tree		2 / 5 / 4
	Driver			
9	L, Bad Pull	G		2 / 5 / 5
	Driver	6 I 175-180 w/wind	10 ft	42

SCORE

IN

10	
11	
12	
13	
14	
15	
16	
17	
18	

BIRDIES	0	# GREENS IN		NOTES FOR NEXT PRACTICE SESSION: Rythm
PARS	5	REGULATION	6	on all swings including
BOGEYS	4	# PUTTS	21	putting.
DOUBLE BOGEYS	1	# TEE SHOTS HIT	1	

SCORE

42

TOTAL SCORE

PLAY

COURSE Diamond Oaks, Roseville, CA

	TEE SHOT-HIT FAIRWAY(F), OR MISSED LEFT (L), RIGHT (R)	GREEN IN REGULATION (G), MISSED LEFT (L), MISSED RIGHT (R)	up/down	# OF PUTTS / SCORE / PAR
OUT				
1	R, Push Slice	R, Slice		2 6 / 4
	Drive	3W		15 ft
2	F, Gently Fade	Long w/wind	Y	1 4 / 4
	Drive	SW 50-60 yds		5 ft
3	Par 3	G		2 / 3 / 3
		9 I		30 ft
4	R, Fade	G		3 / 3 / 5
	D	7 I		30 ft
5	R, Bad Slice	Short - Ruff 3 shots to git out		2 / 8 / 4
		4 I		
6	Par 3	Long w/wind	N	2 / 4 / 3
		7 I		
7	F Straight	R, Push	Y	1 / 4 / 5
	D	6 I 180 yds		1 ft
8	R, Push Slice	Long	N	2 / 5 / 4
	D	6 I 150 yd A/wind		3 ft
9	L, Pull	L Putt from Rut	N	2 / 5 / 4
	D	4 I		47

		SCORE		
IN	Valley Oak, Visalia, CA			3/18/94
10	LP	Hit tree from fairway trap	N	2 6 / 4
	Driver		SW shot	25 ft
11				
12				
13				
14				
15				
16				
17				
18				

BIRDIES		# GREENS IN	
PARS		REGULATION 2	
BOGEYS		# PUTTS 17	
DOUBLE BOGEYS		# TEE SHOTS HIT 2	

NOTES FOR NEXT PRACTICE SESSION: Putting: Long follow through

SCORE 47

TOTAL SCORE

PLAY

DATE 3/25/94
DAY Friday

COURSE Diamond Oaks   Roseville, CA   RATING/SLOPE 68.2 / 110

	TEE SHOT-HIT FAIRWAY(F), OR MISSED LEFT (L), RIGHT (R)	GREEN IN REGULATION (G), MISSED LEFT (L), MISSED RIGHT (R)	# OF PUTTS / SCORE / PAR
OUT			
1	R, Push	G	2 / 5 / 5
	Driver		
2	R, Push	Short	2 / 4 / 4
	D	7 I	
3	Par 3	G	2 / 3 / 3
	9 I		
4	R, Push	G	2 / 4 / 4
	D		
5	R, Push Slice	Long, Hit thin	1 / 5 / 4
	D	8 I	
6	Par 3	G	2 / 3 / 3
	8 I		
7	F	G	2 / 4 / 5
	D		
8	P, Push Slice	Short	2 / 5 / 4
	D	7 I	
9	F	L	3 / 7 / 4
	D	2 I	**40**
			SCORE

IN

10

11

12

13

14

15

16

17

18

BIRDIES _1_   # GREENS IN

PARS _5_   REGULATION _4_

BOGEYS _2_   # PUTTS _18_

Triple
~~DOUBLE~~ BOGEYS _3_   # TEE SHOTS HIT _4_

NOTES FOR NEXT PRACTICE SESSION: Driver
Sand Wedge

SCORE

TOTAL SCORE

PLAY

COURSE _____ Diamond Oaks _____

	TEE SHOT-HIT FAIRWAY(F), OR MISSED LEFT (L), RIGHT (R)	GREEN IN REGULATION (G), MISSED LEFT (L), MISSED RIGHT (R)	# OF PUTTS / SCORE / PAR

OUT

1

2

3

4

5

6

7

8

9

IN   SCORE

10			1	4/4
11			2	7/5
12			1	3/3
13			2	5/4
14			2	3/3
15			2	6/5
16			2	5/4
17			2	5/4
18			2	4/4

SCORE 41

BIRDIES	0	# GREENS IN		NOTES FOR NEXT PRACTICE SESSION:	SCORE
PARS	5	REGULATION	3		
BOGEYS		# PUTTS	16		TOTAL SCORE
DOUBLE BOGEYS		# TEE SHOTS HIT	4		

PLAY

DATE _____

DAY _____

COURSE _____ RATING/SLOPE _____

| | TEE SHOT-HIT FAIRWAY(F), OR MISSED LEFT (L), RIGHT (R) | GREEN IN REGULATION (G), MISSED LEFT (L), MISSED RIGHT (R) | # OF PUTTS / SCORE / PAR |

OUT

1

2

3

4

5

6

7

8

9

SCORE

IN

10

11

12

13

14

15

16

17

18

BIRDIES _____	# GREENS IN	NOTES FOR NEXT PRACTICE SESSION: _____	
PARS _____	REGULATION _____	_____	**SCORE**
BOGEYS_____	# PUTTS _____	_____	
DOUBLE BOGEYS _____	# TEE SHOTS HIT_____	_____	**TOTAL SCORE**

PLAY

DATE _____

DAY _____

COURSE _____ RATING/SLOPE _____

| | TEE SHOT-HIT FAIRWAY(F), OR MISSED LEFT (L), RIGHT (R) | GREEN IN REGULATION (G), MISSED LEFT (L), MISSED RIGHT (R) | # OF PUTTS / SCORE / PAR |

OUT

1 _____

2 _____

3 _____

4 _____

5 _____

6 _____

7 _____

8 _____

9 _____

SCORE

IN

10 _____

11 _____

12 _____

13 _____

14 _____

15 _____

16 _____

17 _____

18 _____

BIRDIES _____   # GREENS IN

PARS _____   REGULATION _____

BOGEYS _____   # PUTTS _____

DOUBLE BOGEYS _____   # TEE SHOTS HIT _____

NOTES FOR NEXT PRACTICE SESSION: _____
_____
_____

SCORE

TOTAL SCORE

LAY

DATE _____

DAY _____

COURSE _____ RATING/SLOPE _____

| | TEE SHOT-HIT FAIRWAY(F), OR MISSED LEFT (L), RIGHT (R) | GREEN IN REGULATION (G), MISSED LEFT (L), MISSED RIGHT (R) | # OF PUTTS / SCORE / PAR |

OUT

1 _____

2 _____

3 _____

4 _____

5 _____

6 _____

7 _____

8 _____

9 _____

SCORE

IN

10 _____

11 _____

12 _____

13 _____

14 _____

15 _____

16 _____

17 _____

18 _____

BIRDIES _____   # GREENS IN

PARS _____   REGULATION _____   NOTES FOR NEXT PRACTICE SESSION: _____   **SCORE**

BOGEYS _____   # PUTTS _____

DOUBLE BOGEYS _____   # TEE SHOTS HIT_____   **TOTAL SCORE**

PLAY

DATE _____

DAY _____

COURSE _____ RATING/SLOPE _____

| | TEE SHOT-HIT FAIRWAY(F), OR MISSED LEFT (L), RIGHT (R) | GREEN IN REGULATION (G), MISSED LEFT (L), MISSED RIGHT (R) | # OF PUTTS / SCORE / PAR |

OUT

1 _____

2 _____

3 _____

4 _____

5 _____

6 _____

7 _____

8 _____

9 _____

SCORE

IN

10 _____

11 _____

12 _____

13 _____

14 _____

15 _____

16 _____

17 _____

18 _____

BIRDIES _____ # GREENS IN   NOTES FOR NEXT PRACTICE SESSION: _____

PARS _____ REGULATION _____   _____ **SCORE**

BOGEYS _____ # PUTTS _____   _____

DOUBLE BOGEYS _____ # TEE SHOTS HIT_____   _____ **TOTAL SCORE**

LAY

DATE _____

DAY _____

COURSE _____ RATING/SLOPE_____

| | TEE SHOT-HIT FAIRWAY(F),
OR MISSED LEFT (L), RIGHT (R) | GREEN IN REGULATION (G),
MISSED LEFT (L), MISSED RIGHT (R) | # OF PUTTS / SCORE / PAR |

OUT

1 _____

2 _____

3 _____

4 _____

5 _____

6 _____

7 _____

8 _____

9 _____

SCORE

IN

10 _____

11 _____

12 _____

13 _____

14 _____

15 _____

16 _____

17 _____

18 _____

BIRDIES _____ # GREENS IN NOTES FOR NEXT PRACTICE SESSION: _____

PARS _____ REGULATION _____ _____ **SCORE**

BOGEYS_____ # PUTTS _____ _____

DOUBLE BOGEYS_____ # TEE SHOTS HIT_____ _____ **TOTAL SCORE**

PLAY

DATE _____

DAY _____

COURSE _____ RATING/SLOPE_____

| | TEE SHOT-HIT FAIRWAY(F), OR MISSED LEFT (L), RIGHT (R) | GREEN IN REGULATION (G), MISSED LEFT (L), MISSED RIGHT (R) | # OF PUTTS / SCORE / PAR |

OUT

1

2

3

4

5

6

7

8

9

SCORE

IN

10

11

12

13

14

15

16

17

18

BIRDIES _____   # GREENS IN

PARS _____   REGULATION _____

BOGEYS _____   # PUTTS _____

DOUBLE BOGEYS _____   # TEE SHOTS HIT _____

NOTES FOR NEXT PRACTICE SESSION: _____

_____

_____

_____

SCORE

TOTAL SCORE

PLAY

DATE _____

DAY _____

COURSE _____ RATING/SLOPE_____

| | TEE SHOT-HIT FAIRWAY(F), OR MISSED LEFT (L), RIGHT (R) | GREEN IN REGULATION (G), MISSED LEFT (L), MISSED RIGHT (R) | # OF PUTTS / SCORE / PAR |

OUT

1

2

3

4

5

6

7

8

9

SCORE

IN

10

11

12

13

14

15

16

17

18

BIRDIES _____   # GREENS IN ·

PARS _____   REGULATION _____   **SCORE**

BOGEYS _____   # PUTTS _____

DOUBLE BOGEYS _____   # TEE SHOTS HIT_____

NOTES FOR NEXT PRACTICE SESSION: _____

_____

_____

_____

TOTAL SCORE

LAY

DATE _____

DAY _____

COURSE _____ RATING/SLOPE _____

| | TEE SHOT-HIT FAIRWAY(F), OR MISSED LEFT (L), RIGHT (R) | GREEN IN REGULATION (G), MISSED LEFT (L), MISSED RIGHT (R) | # OF PUTTS / SCORE / PAR |

OUT

1

2

3

4

5

6

7

8

9

SCORE

IN

10

11

12

13

14

15

16

17

18

BIRDIES _____   # GREENS IN _____   NOTES FOR NEXT PRACTICE SESSION: _____

PARS _____   REGULATION _____   _____   **SCORE**

BOGEYS _____   # PUTTS _____   _____

DOUBLE BOGEYS _____   # TEE SHOTS HIT_____   _____   **TOTAL SCORE**

"I'm hitting the woods just great. But I'm having a terrible time hitting out of them."

-Harry Toscano, Pro

"What other people may find in poetry
or art museums, I find in the flight
of a good drive."

-Arnold Palmer

LAY

DATE _____

DAY _____

COURSE _____ RATING/SLOPE_____

| | TEE SHOT-HIT FAIRWAY(F), OR MISSED LEFT (L), RIGHT (R) | GREEN IN REGULATION (G), MISSED LEFT (L), MISSED RIGHT (R) | # OF PUTTS / SCORE / PAR |

OUT

1 _____

2 _____

3 _____

4 _____

5 _____

6 _____

7 _____

8 _____

9 _____

SCORE

IN

10 _____

11 _____

12 _____

13 _____

14 _____

15 _____

16 _____

17 _____

18 _____

BIRDIES _____	# GREENS IN	NOTES FOR NEXT PRACTICE SESSION: _____	
PARS _____	REGULATION _____	_____	**SCORE**
BOGEYS_____	# PUTTS _____	_____	
DOUBLE BOGEYS _____	# TEE SHOTS HIT_____	_____	**TOTAL SCORE**

PLAY

DATE _____

DAY _____

COURSE _____ RATING/SLOPE _____

	TEE SHOT-HIT FAIRWAY(F), OR MISSED LEFT (L), RIGHT (R)	GREEN IN REGULATION (G), MISSED LEFT (L), MISSED RIGHT (R)	# OF PUTTS / SCORE / PAR

OUT

1

2

3

4

5

6

7

8

9

SCORE

IN

10

11

12

13

14

15

16

17

18

BIRDIES _____   # GREENS IN   NOTES FOR NEXT PRACTICE SESSION: _____   **SCORE**

PARS _____   REGULATION _____

BOGEYS _____   # PUTTS _____

DOUBLE BOGEYS _____   # TEE SHOTS HIT _____   **TOTAL SCORE**

PLAY

COURSE _____ RATING/SLOPE_____

	TEE SHOT-HIT FAIRWAY(F), OR MISSED LEFT (L), RIGHT (R)	GREEN IN REGULATION (G), MISSED LEFT (L), MISSED RIGHT (R)	# OF PUTTS / SCORE / PAR

OUT

1

2

3

4

5

6

7

8

9

SCORE

IN

10

11

12

13

14

15

16

17

18

BIRDIES _____	# GREENS IN	NOTES FOR NEXT PRACTICE SESSION: _____	**SCORE**
PARS _____	REGULATION _____	_____	
BOGEYS_____	# PUTTS _____	_____	
DOUBLE BOGEYS_____	# TEE SHOTS HIT_____	_____	**TOTAL SCORE**

LAY

DATE _____

DAY _____

COURSE _____ RATING/SLOPE _____

	TEE SHOT-HIT FAIRWAY(F), OR MISSED LEFT (L), RIGHT (R)	GREEN IN REGULATION (G), MISSED LEFT (L), MISSED RIGHT (R)	# OF PUTTS / SCORE / PAR

OUT

1 _____

2 _____

3 _____

4 _____

5 _____

6 _____

7 _____

8 _____

9 _____

SCORE

IN

10 _____

11 _____

12 _____

13 _____

14 _____

15 _____

16 _____

17 _____

18 _____

BIRDIES _____	# GREENS IN	NOTES FOR NEXT PRACTICE SESSION: _____	
PARS _____	REGULATION _____	_____	**SCORE**
BOGEYS _____	# PUTTS _____	_____	
DOUBLE BOGEYS _____	# TEE SHOTS HIT _____	_____	**TOTAL SCORE**

PLAY

DATE _____

DAY _____

COURSE _____ RATING/SLOPE_____

	TEE SHOT-HIT FAIRWAY(F), OR MISSED LEFT (L), RIGHT (R)	GREEN IN REGULATION (G), MISSED LEFT (L), MISSED RIGHT (R)	# OF PUTTS / SCORE / PAR

OUT

1

2

3

4

5

6

7

8

9

SCORE

IN

10

11

12

13

14

15

16

17

18

BIRDIES _____	# GREENS IN	NOTES FOR NEXT PRACTICE SESSION: _____	
PARS _____	REGULATION _____	_____	**SCORE**
BOGEYS_____	# PUTTS _____	_____	
DOUBLE BOGEYS _____	# TEE SHOTS HIT_____	_____	**TOTAL SCORE**

PLAY

DATE _____

DAY _____

COURSE _____ RATING/SLOPE _____

| | TEE SHOT-HIT FAIRWAY(F),
OR MISSED LEFT (L), RIGHT (R) | GREEN IN REGULATION (G),
MISSED LEFT (L), MISSED RIGHT (R) | # OF PUTTS / SCORE / PAR |

OUT

1

2

3

4

5

6

7

8

9

SCORE

IN

10

11

12

13

14

15

16

17

18

BIRDIES _____	# GREENS IN	NOTES FOR NEXT PRACTICE SESSION: _____	
PARS _____	REGULATION _____	_____	**SCORE**
BOGEYS _____	# PUTTS _____	_____	
DOUBLE BOGEYS _____	# TEE SHOTS HIT _____	_____	**TOTAL SCORE**

PLAY

DATE _____

DAY _____

COURSE _____ RATING/SLOPE _____

| | TEE SHOT-HIT FAIRWAY(F), OR MISSED LEFT (L), RIGHT (R) | GREEN IN REGULATION (G), MISSED LEFT (L), MISSED RIGHT (R) | # OF PUTTS / SCORE / PAR |

OUT

1 _____

2 _____

3 _____

4 _____

5 _____

6 _____

7 _____

8 _____

9 _____

SCORE

IN

10 _____

11 _____

12 _____

13 _____

14 _____

15 _____

16 _____

17 _____

18 _____

BIRDIES _____   # GREENS IN   NOTES FOR NEXT PRACTICE SESSION: _____

PARS _____   REGULATION _____   **SCORE**

BOGEYS_____   # PUTTS _____   _____

DOUBLE BOGEYS _____   # TEE SHOTS HIT_____   _____   **TOTAL SCORE**

LAY

DATE _____

DAY _____

COURSE _____ RATING/SLOPE_____

| | TEE SHOT-HIT FAIRWAY(F), OR MISSED LEFT (L), RIGHT (R) | GREEN IN REGULATION (G), MISSED LEFT (L), MISSED RIGHT (R) | # OF PUTTS / SCORE / PAR |

OUT

1

2

3

4

5

6

7

8

9

SCORE

IN

10

11

12

13

14

15

16

17

18

BIRDIES _____   # GREENS IN

PARS _____   REGULATION _____   NOTES FOR NEXT PRACTICE SESSION: _____   **SCORE**

BOGEYS_____   # PUTTS _____

DOUBLE BOGEYS _____   # TEE SHOTS HIT_____   **TOTAL SCORE**

PLAY

DATE _____

DAY _____

COURSE _____ RATING/SLOPE_____

	TEE SHOT-HIT FAIRWAY(F), OR MISSED LEFT (L), RIGHT (R)	GREEN IN REGULATION (G), MISSED LEFT (L), MISSED RIGHT (R)	# OF PUTTS / SCORE / PAR

OUT

1

2

3

4

5

6

7

8

9

SCORE

IN

10

11

12

13

14

15

16

17

18

SCORE

BIRDIES _____	# GREENS IN	NOTES FOR NEXT PRACTICE SESSION: _____
PARS _____	REGULATION _____	
BOGEYS_____	# PUTTS _____	
DOUBLE BOGEYS _____	# TEE SHOTS HIT_____	

TOTAL SCORE

LAY

DATE _____

DAY _____

COURSE _____ RATING/SLOPE_____

| | TEE SHOT-HIT FAIRWAY(F), OR MISSED LEFT (L), RIGHT (R) | GREEN IN REGULATION (G), MISSED LEFT (L), MISSED RIGHT (R) | # OF PUTTS / SCORE / PAR |

OUT

1 _____

2 _____

3 _____

4 _____

5 _____

6 _____

7 _____

8 _____

9 _____

SCORE

IN

10 _____

11 _____

12 _____

13 _____

14 _____

15 _____

16 _____

17 _____

18 _____

BIRDIES _____   # GREENS IN   NOTES FOR NEXT PRACTICE SESSION: _____

PARS _____   REGULATION _____   _____   **SCORE**

BOGEYS _____   # PUTTS _____   _____

DOUBLE BOGEYS _____   # TEE SHOTS HIT_____   _____   **TOTAL SCORE**

PLAY

DATE _____

DAY _____

COURSE _____ RATING/SLOPE_____

	TEE SHOT-HIT FAIRWAY(F), OR MISSED LEFT (L), RIGHT (R)	GREEN IN REGULATION (G), MISSED LEFT (L), MISSED RIGHT (R)	# OF PUTTS / SCORE / PAR

OUT

1

2

3

4

5

6

7

8

9

SCORE

IN

10

11

12

13

14

15

16

17

18

BIRDIES _____   # GREENS IN

PARS _____   REGULATION _____   NOTES FOR NEXT PRACTICE SESSION: _____

BOGEYS _____   # PUTTS _____

DOUBLE BOGEYS _____   # TEE SHOTS HIT_____

SCORE

TOTAL SCORE

PLAY

COURSE _____ RATING/SLOPE_____

	TEE SHOT-HIT FAIRWAY(F), OR MISSED LEFT (L), RIGHT (R)	GREEN IN REGULATION (G), MISSED LEFT (L), MISSED RIGHT (R)	# OF PUTTS / SCORE / PAR

OUT

1

2

3

4

5

6

7

8

9

SCORE

IN

10

11

12

13

14

15

16

17

18

BIRDIES _____	# GREENS IN	NOTES FOR NEXT PRACTICE SESSION: _____	
PARS _____	REGULATION _____	·	**SCORE**
BOGEYS_____	# PUTTS _____	_____	
DOUBLE BOGEYS _____	# TEE SHOTS HIT_____	_____	**TOTAL SCORE**

LAY

DATE _____

DAY _____

COURSE _____ RATING/SLOPE _____

| | TEE SHOT-HIT FAIRWAY(F), OR MISSED LEFT (L), RIGHT (R) | GREEN IN REGULATION (G), MISSED LEFT (L), MISSED RIGHT (R) | # OF PUTTS / SCORE / PAR |

OUT

1 _____

2 _____

3 _____

4 _____

5 _____

6 _____

7 _____

8 _____

9 _____

SCORE

IN

10 _____

11 _____

12 _____

13 _____

14 _____

15 _____

16 _____

17 _____

18 _____

BIRDIES _____   # GREENS IN

PARS _____   REGULATION _____   **SCORE**

BOGEYS _____   # PUTTS _____

DOUBLE BOGEYS _____   # TEE SHOTS HIT_____   **TOTAL SCORE**

NOTES FOR NEXT PRACTICE SESSION: _____

LAY

DATE _____

DAY _____

COURSE _____ RATING/SLOPE _____

	TEE SHOT-HIT FAIRWAY(F), OR MISSED LEFT (L), RIGHT (R)	GREEN IN REGULATION (G), MISSED LEFT (L), MISSED RIGHT (R)	# OF PUTTS / SCORE / PAR

OUT

1

2

3

4

5

6

7

8

9

SCORE

IN

10

11

12

13

14

15

16

17

18

BIRDIES _____	# GREENS IN	NOTES FOR NEXT PRACTICE SESSION: _____	**SCORE**
PARS _____	REGULATION _____	_____	
BOGEYS_____	# PUTTS _____	_____	
DOUBLE BOGEYS _____	# TEE SHOTS HIT_____	_____	**TOTAL SCORE**

"One of the advantages
bowling has over golf
is that you seldom lose a bowling ball."

-Don Carter, bowling great

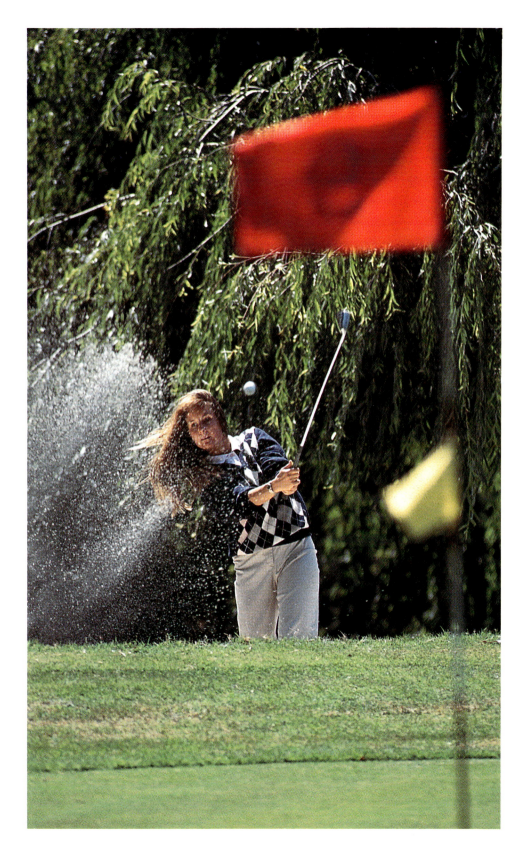

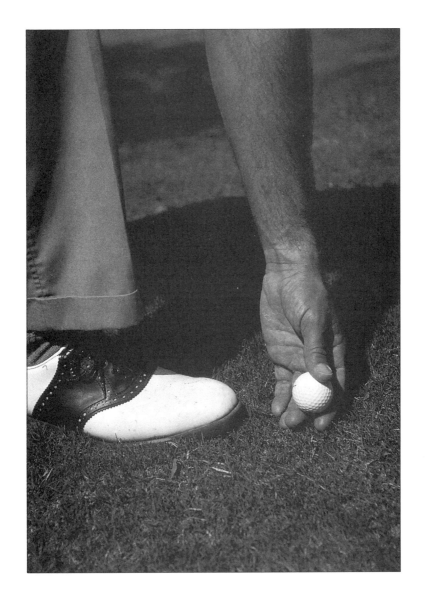

*"Golf is a game in which you yell 'fore,'
shoot six, and write down five."*

-Paul Harvey, news commentator

PLAY

DATE _____

DAY _____

COURSE _____ RATING/SLOPE_____

| | TEE SHOT-HIT FAIRWAY(F), OR MISSED LEFT (L), RIGHT (R) | GREEN IN REGULATION (G), MISSED LEFT (L), MISSED RIGHT (R) | # OF PUTTS / SCORE / PAR |

OUT

1
2
3
4
5
6
7
8
9

SCORE

IN

10
11
12
13
14
15
16
17
18

BIRDIES _____   # GREENS IN

PARS _____   REGULATION _____   NOTES FOR NEXT PRACTICE SESSION: _____

BOGEYS _____   # PUTTS _____   **SCORE**

DOUBLE BOGEYS _____   # TEE SHOTS HIT_____   **TOTAL SCORE**

PLAY

DATE _____
DAY _____

COURSE _____ RATING/SLOPE _____

| | TEE SHOT-HIT FAIRWAY(F), OR MISSED LEFT (L), RIGHT (R) | GREEN IN REGULATION (G), MISSED LEFT (L), MISSED RIGHT (R) | # OF PUTTS / SCORE / PAR |

OUT

1
2
3
4
5
6
7
8
9

SCORE

IN

10
11
12
13
14
15
16
17
18

BIRDIES _____   # GREENS IN
PARS _____   REGULATION _____   NOTES FOR NEXT PRACTICE SESSION: _____   **SCORE**
BOGEYS _____   # PUTTS _____
DOUBLE BOGEYS _____   # TEE SHOTS HIT _____   **TOTAL SCORE**

PLAY

DATE _____

DAY _____

COURSE _____ RATING/SLOPE_____

	TEE SHOT-HIT FAIRWAY(F), OR MISSED LEFT (L), RIGHT (R)	GREEN IN REGULATION (G), MISSED LEFT (L), MISSED RIGHT (R)	# OF PUTTS / SCORE / PAR

OUT

1

2

3

4

5

6

7

8

9

SCORE

IN

10

11

12

13

14

15

16

17

18

BIRDIES _____   # GREENS IN

PARS _____   REGULATION _____   NOTES FOR NEXT PRACTICE SESSION: _____

SCORE

BOGEYS _____   # PUTTS _____

DOUBLE BOGEYS _____   # TEE SHOTS HIT_____

TOTAL SCORE

PLAY

DATE _____

DAY _____

COURSE _____ RATING/SLOPE _____

	TEE SHOT-HIT FAIRWAY(F), OR MISSED LEFT (L), RIGHT (R)	GREEN IN REGULATION (G), MISSED LEFT (L), MISSED RIGHT (R)	# OF PUTTS / SCORE / PAR

OUT

1

2

3

4

5

6

7

8

9

SCORE

IN

10

11

12

13

14

15

16

17

18

BIRDIES _____   # GREENS IN   NOTES FOR NEXT PRACTICE SESSION: _____   **SCORE**

PARS _____   REGULATION _____   _____

BOGEYS _____   # PUTTS _____   _____

DOUBLE BOGEYS _____   # TEE SHOTS HIT _____   _____   **TOTAL SCORE**

COURSE _____

DATE _____
DAY _____
RATING/SLOPE _____

| | TEE SHOT-HIT FAIRWAY(F), OR MISSED LEFT (L), RIGHT (R) | GREEN IN REGULATION (G), MISSED LEFT (L), MISSED RIGHT (R) | # OF PUTTS / SCORE / PAR |

OUT

1
2
3
4
5
6
7
8
9

SCORE

IN

10
11
12
13
14
15
16
17
18

BIRDIES _____
PARS _____
BOGEYS _____
DOUBLE BOGEYS _____

GREENS IN
REGULATION _____
PUTTS _____
TEE SHOTS HIT _____

NOTES FOR NEXT PRACTICE SESSION: _____
_____
_____
_____

SCORE

TOTAL SCORE

LAY

DATE _____

DAY _____

COURSE _____ RATING/SLOPE _____

	TEE SHOT-HIT FAIRWAY(F), OR MISSED LEFT (L), RIGHT (R)	GREEN IN REGULATION (G), MISSED LEFT (L), MISSED RIGHT (R)	# OF PUTTS / SCORE / PAR

OUT

1

2

3

4

5

6

7

8

9

SCORE

IN

10

11

12

13

14

15

16

17

18

BIRDIES _____	# GREENS IN	NOTES FOR NEXT PRACTICE SESSION: _____	**SCORE**
PARS _____	REGULATION _____	_____	
BOGEYS _____	# PUTTS _____	_____	
DOUBLE BOGEYS _____	# TEE SHOTS HIT _____	_____	**TOTAL SCORE**

LAY

DATE _____

DAY _____

COURSE _____ RATING/SLOPE_____

	TEE SHOT-HIT FAIRWAY(F), OR MISSED LEFT (L), RIGHT (R)	GREEN IN REGULATION (G), MISSED LEFT (L), MISSED RIGHT (R)	# OF PUTTS / SCORE / PAR

OUT

1 _____

2 _____

3 _____

4 _____

5 _____

6 _____

7 _____

8 _____

9 _____

SCORE

IN

10 _____

11 _____

12 _____

13 _____

14 _____

15 _____

16 _____

17 _____

18 _____

BIRDIES _____ # GREENS IN   NOTES FOR NEXT PRACTICE SESSION: _____

PARS _____ REGULATION _____ _____ **SCORE**

BOGEYS_____ # PUTTS _____ _____

DOUBLE BOGEYS _____ # TEE SHOTS HIT_____ _____ **TOTAL SCORE**

LAY

DATE _____

DAY _____

COURSE _____ RATING/SLOPE_____

	TEE SHOT-HIT FAIRWAY(F), OR MISSED LEFT (L), RIGHT (R)	GREEN IN REGULATION (G), MISSED LEFT (L), MISSED RIGHT (R)	# OF PUTTS / SCORE / PAR

OUT

1 _____

2 _____

3 _____

4 _____

5 _____

6 _____

7 _____

8 _____

9 _____

SCORE

IN

10 _____

11 _____

12 _____

13 _____

14 _____

15 _____

16 _____

17 _____

18 _____

BIRDIES _____	# GREENS IN	NOTES FOR NEXT PRACTICE SESSION: _____	**SCORE**
PARS _____	REGULATION _____	_____	
BOGEYS _____	# PUTTS _____	_____	
DOUBLE BOGEYS _____	# TEE SHOTS HIT_____	_____	**TOTAL SCORE**

LAY

DATE _____

DAY _____

COURSE _____ RATING/SLOPE _____

| | TEE SHOT-HIT FAIRWAY(F), OR MISSED LEFT (L), RIGHT (R) | GREEN IN REGULATION (G), MISSED LEFT (L), MISSED RIGHT (R) | # OF PUTTS / SCORE / PAR |

OUT

1

2

3

4

5

6

7

8

9

SCORE

IN

10

11

12

13

14

15

16

17

18

BIRDIES _____	# GREENS IN	NOTES FOR NEXT PRACTICE SESSION: _____	
PARS _____	REGULATION _____	_____	**SCORE**
BOGEYS_____	# PUTTS _____	_____	
DOUBLE BOGEYS _____	# TEE SHOTS HIT_____	_____	**TOTAL SCORE**

PLAY

DATE _____

DAY _____

COURSE _____ RATING/SLOPE _____

| | TEE SHOT-HIT FAIRWAY(F), OR MISSED LEFT (L), RIGHT (R) | GREEN IN REGULATION (G), MISSED LEFT (L), MISSED RIGHT (R) | # OF PUTTS / SCORE / PAR |

OUT

1

2

3

4

5

6

7

8

9

SCORE

IN

10

11

12

13

14

15

16

17

18

BIRDIES _____   # GREENS IN

PARS _____   REGULATION _____

BOGEYS _____   # PUTTS _____

DOUBLE BOGEYS _____   # TEE SHOTS HIT_____

NOTES FOR NEXT PRACTICE SESSION: _____

_____

_____

_____

SCORE

TOTAL SCORE

LAY

DATE _____

DAY _____

COURSE _____ RATING/SLOPE _____

| | TEE SHOT-HIT FAIRWAY(F), OR MISSED LEFT (L), RIGHT (R) | GREEN IN REGULATION (G), MISSED LEFT (L), MISSED RIGHT (R) | # OF PUTTS / SCORE / PAR |

OUT

1 _____

2 _____

3 _____

4 _____

5 _____

6 _____

7 _____

8 _____

9 _____

SCORE

IN

10 _____

11 _____

12 _____

13 _____

14 _____

15 _____

16 _____

17 _____

18 _____

BIRDIES _____   # GREENS IN

PARS _____   REGULATION _____

BOGEYS _____   # PUTTS _____

DOUBLE BOGEYS _____   # TEE SHOTS HIT _____

NOTES FOR NEXT PRACTICE SESSION: _____

_____

_____

SCORE

TOTAL SCORE

PLAY

DATE _____

DAY _____

COURSE _____ RATING/SLOPE _____

| | TEE SHOT-HIT FAIRWAY(F), OR MISSED LEFT (L), RIGHT (R) | GREEN IN REGULATION (G), MISSED LEFT (L), MISSED RIGHT (R) | # OF PUTTS / SCORE / PAR |

OUT

1

2

3

4

5

6

7

8

9

SCORE

IN

10

11

12

13

14

15

16

17

18

BIRDIES _____	# GREENS IN	NOTES FOR NEXT PRACTICE SESSION: _____	
PARS _____	REGULATION _____	_____	**SCORE**
BOGEYS _____	# PUTTS _____	_____	
DOUBLE BOGEYS _____	# TEE SHOTS HIT _____	_____	**TOTAL SCORE**

PLAY

DATE _____
DAY _____

COURSE _____ RATING/SLOPE_____

| | TEE SHOT-HIT FAIRWAY(F), OR MISSED LEFT (L), RIGHT (R) | GREEN IN REGULATION (G), MISSED LEFT (L), MISSED RIGHT (R) | # OF PUTTS / SCORE / PAR |

OUT

1

2

3

4

5

6

7

8

9

SCORE

IN

10

11

12

13

14

15

16

17

18

BIRDIES _____   # GREENS IN

PARS _____   REGULATION _____   NOTES FOR NEXT PRACTICE SESSION: _____   **SCORE**

BOGEYS_____   # PUTTS _____

DOUBLE BOGEYS _____   # TEE SHOTS HIT_____   **TOTAL SCORE**

LAY

DATE _____

DAY _____

COURSE _____ RATING/SLOPE _____

	TEE SHOT-HIT FAIRWAY(F), OR MISSED LEFT (L), RIGHT (R)	GREEN IN REGULATION (G), MISSED LEFT (L), MISSED RIGHT (R)	# OF PUTTS / SCORE / PAR

OUT

1

2

3

4

5

6

7

8

9

SCORE

IN

10

11

12

13

14

15

16

17

18

BIRDIES _____ # GREENS IN

PARS _____ REGULATION _____ NOTES FOR NEXT PRACTICE SESSION: _____

BOGEYS _____ # PUTTS _____ **SCORE**

DOUBLE BOGEYS _____ # TEE SHOTS HIT _____

TOTAL SCORE

"The devoted golfer is an anguished soul
who has learned a lot about putting
just as an avalanche victim
has learned a lot about snow."

-Dan Jenkins, author

"*Golf is a good walk spoiled.*"

-Mark Twain

LAY

DATE _____

DAY _____

COURSE _____ RATING/SLOPE_____

| | TEE SHOT-HIT FAIRWAY(F), OR MISSED LEFT (L), RIGHT (R) | GREEN IN REGULATION (G), MISSED LEFT (L), MISSED RIGHT (R) | # OF PUTTS / SCORE / PAR |

OUT

1 _____

2 _____

3 _____

4 _____

5 _____

6 _____

7 _____

8 _____

9 _____

SCORE

IN

10 _____

11 _____

12 _____

13 _____

14 _____

15 _____

16 _____

17 _____

18 _____

BIRDIES _____ # GREENS IN

PARS _____ REGULATION _____ NOTES FOR NEXT PRACTICE SESSION: _____

BOGEYS_____ # PUTTS _____ **SCORE**

DOUBLE BOGEYS_____ # TEE SHOTS HIT_____ **TOTAL SCORE**

LAY

DATE _____

DAY _____

COURSE _____ RATING/SLOPE_____

	TEE SHOT-HIT FAIRWAY(F), OR MISSED LEFT (L), RIGHT (R)	GREEN IN REGULATION (G), MISSED LEFT (L), MISSED RIGHT (R)	# OF PUTTS / SCORE / PAR

OUT

1

2

3

4

5

6

7

8

9

SCORE

IN

10

11

12

13

14

15

16

17

18

BIRDIES _____	# GREENS IN	NOTES FOR NEXT PRACTICE SESSION: _____	
PARS _____	REGULATION _____	_____	**SCORE**
BOGEYS _____	# PUTTS _____	_____	
DOUBLE BOGEYS _____	# TEE SHOTS HIT_____	_____	**TOTAL SCORE**

PLAY

DATE _____

DAY _____

COURSE _____ RATING/SLOPE _____

| | TEE SHOT-HIT FAIRWAY(F), OR MISSED LEFT (L), RIGHT (R) | GREEN IN REGULATION (G), MISSED LEFT (L), MISSED RIGHT (R) | # OF PUTTS / SCORE / PAR |

OUT

1 _____

2 _____

3 _____

4 _____

5 _____

6 _____

7 _____

8 _____

9 _____

SCORE

IN

10 _____

11 _____

12 _____

13 _____

14 _____

15 _____

16 _____

17 _____

18 _____

BIRDIES _____	# GREENS IN	NOTES FOR NEXT PRACTICE SESSION: _____	**SCORE**
PARS _____	REGULATION _____	_____	
BOGEYS _____	# PUTTS _____	_____	
DOUBLE BOGEYS _____	# TEE SHOTS HIT _____	_____	**TOTAL SCORE**

LAY

DATE _____

DAY _____

COURSE _____ RATING/SLOPE_____

	TEE SHOT-HIT FAIRWAY(F), OR MISSED LEFT (L), RIGHT (R)	GREEN IN REGULATION (G), MISSED LEFT (L), MISSED RIGHT (R)	# OF PUTTS / SCORE / PAR

OUT

1

2

3

4

5

6

7

8

9

SCORE

IN

10

11

12

13

14

15

16

17

18

BIRDIES _____ # GREENS IN NOTES FOR NEXT PRACTICE SESSION: _____

PARS _____ REGULATION _____ _____ **SCORE**

BOGEYS_____ # PUTTS _____ _____

DOUBLE BOGEYS _____ # TEE SHOTS HIT_____ _____ **TOTAL SCORE**

PLAY

DATE _____
DAY _____

COURSE _____ RATING/SLOPE_____

| | TEE SHOT-HIT FAIRWAY(F), OR MISSED LEFT (L), RIGHT (R) | GREEN IN REGULATION (G), MISSED LEFT (L), MISSED RIGHT (R) | # OF PUTTS / SCORE / PAR |

OUT

1

2

3

4

5

6

7

8

9

SCORE

IN

10

11

12

13

14

15

16

17

18

BIRDIES _____ # GREENS IN NOTES FOR NEXT PRACTICE SESSION: _____
PARS _____ REGULATION _____ **SCORE**
BOGEYS_____ # PUTTS _____
DOUBLE BOGEYS _____ # TEE SHOTS HIT_____ **TOTAL SCORE**

LAY

DATE _____

DAY _____

COURSE _____ RATING/SLOPE_____

| | TEE SHOT-HIT FAIRWAY(F), OR MISSED LEFT (L), RIGHT (R) | GREEN IN REGULATION (G), MISSED LEFT (L), MISSED RIGHT (R) | # OF PUTTS / SCORE / PAR |

OUT

1 _____

2 _____

3 _____

4 _____

5 _____

6 _____

7 _____

8 _____

9 _____

SCORE

IN

10 _____

11 _____

12 _____

13 _____

14 _____

15 _____

16 _____

17 _____

18 _____

BIRDIES _____ # GREENS IN

PARS _____ REGULATION _____

BOGEYS_____ # PUTTS _____

DOUBLE BOGEYS _____ # TEE SHOTS HIT_____

NOTES FOR NEXT PRACTICE SESSION: _____

_____

_____

_____

SCORE

TOTAL SCORE

PLAY

DATE _____

DAY _____

COURSE _____ RATING/SLOPE_____

| | TEE SHOT-HIT FAIRWAY(F), OR MISSED LEFT (L), RIGHT (R) | GREEN IN REGULATION (G), MISSED LEFT (L), MISSED RIGHT (R) | # OF PUTTS / SCORE / PAR |

OUT

1

2

3

4

5

6

7

8

9

SCORE

IN

10

11

12

13

14

15

16

17

18

SCORE

BIRDIES _____	# GREENS IN	NOTES FOR NEXT PRACTICE SESSION: _____
PARS_____	REGULATION _____	_____
BOGEYS_____	# PUTTS _____	_____
DOUBLE BOGEYS_____	# TEE SHOTS HIT_____	_____

SCORE

TOTAL SCORE

PLAY

DATE _____

DAY _____

COURSE _____ RATING/SLOPE_____

	TEE SHOT-HIT FAIRWAY(F), OR MISSED LEFT (L), RIGHT (R)	GREEN IN REGULATION (G), MISSED LEFT (L), MISSED RIGHT (R)	# OF PUTTS / SCORE / PAR

OUT

1

2

3

4

5

6

7

8

9

SCORE

IN

10

11

12

13

14

15

16

17

18

BIRDIES _____   # GREENS IN   NOTES FOR NEXT PRACTICE SESSION: _____

PARS _____   REGULATION _____   _____   **SCORE**

BOGEYS_____   # PUTTS _____   _____

DOUBLE BOGEYS _____   # TEE SHOTS HIT_____   _____   **TOTAL SCORE**

PLAY

DATE _____

DAY _____

COURSE _____ RATING/SLOPE _____

| | TEE SHOT-HIT FAIRWAY(F), OR MISSED LEFT (L), RIGHT (R) | GREEN IN REGULATION (G), MISSED LEFT (L), MISSED RIGHT (R) | # OF PUTTS / SCORE / PAR |

OUT

1

2

3

4

5

6

7

8

9

SCORE

IN

10

11

12

13

14

15

16

17

18

BIRDIES _____	# GREENS IN	NOTES FOR NEXT PRACTICE SESSION: _____	
PARS _____	REGULATION _____	_____	**SCORE**
BOGEYS _____	# PUTTS _____	_____	
DOUBLE BOGEYS _____	# TEE SHOTS HIT_____	_____	**TOTAL SCORE**

PLAY

COURSE _____

	TEE SHOT-HIT FAIRWAY(F), OR MISSED LEFT (L), RIGHT (R)	GREEN IN REGULATION (G), MISSED LEFT (L), MISSED RIGHT (R)	# OF PUTTS / SCORE / PAR

OUT

1

2

3

4

5

6

7

8

9

SCORE

IN

10

11

12

13

14

15

16

17

18

BIRDIES _____	# GREENS IN	NOTES FOR NEXT PRACTICE SESSION: _____	**SCORE**
PARS _____	REGULATION _____	_____	
BOGEYS _____	# PUTTS _____	_____	
DOUBLE BOGEYS _____	# TEE SHOTS HIT_____	_____	**TOTAL SCORE**

PLAY

DATE _____

DAY _____

COURSE _____ RATING/SLOPE_____

	TEE SHOT-HIT FAIRWAY(F), OR MISSED LEFT (L), RIGHT (R)	GREEN IN REGULATION (G), MISSED LEFT (L), MISSED RIGHT (R)	# OF PUTTS / SCORE / PAR

OUT

1 _____

_____

2 _____

_____

3 _____

_____

4 _____

_____

5 _____

_____

6 _____

_____

7 _____

_____

8 _____

_____

9 _____

_____

SCORE

IN

10 _____

_____

11 _____

_____

12 _____

_____

13 _____

_____

14 _____

_____

15 _____

_____

16 _____

_____

17 _____

_____

18 _____

_____

BIRDIES _____   # GREENS IN   NOTES FOR NEXT PRACTICE SESSION: _____

PARS _____   REGULATION _____   _____   **SCORE**

BOGEYS _____   # PUTTS _____   _____

DOUBLE BOGEYS _____   # TEE SHOTS HIT_____   _____   **TOTAL SCORE**

LAY

DATE _____

DAY _____

COURSE _____ RATING/SLOPE _____

	TEE SHOT-HIT FAIRWAY(F), OR MISSED LEFT (L), RIGHT (R)	GREEN IN REGULATION (G), MISSED LEFT (L), MISSED RIGHT (R)	# OF PUTTS / SCORE / PAR

OUT

1 _____

2 _____

3 _____ •

4 _____

5 _____

6 _____

7 _____

8 _____

9 _____

SCORE

IN

10 _____

11 _____

12 _____

13 _____

14 _____

15 _____

16 _____

17 _____

18 _____

BIRDIES _____ # GREENS IN

PARS _____ REGULATION _____ NOTES FOR NEXT PRACTICE SESSION: _____

BOGEYS _____ # PUTTS _____ **SCORE**

DOUBLE BOGEYS _____ # TEE SHOTS HIT_____ **TOTAL SCORE**

P LAY

DATE _____

DAY _____

COURSE _____ RATING/SLOPE_____

	TEE SHOT-HIT FAIRWAY(F), OR MISSED LEFT (L), RIGHT (R)	GREEN IN REGULATION (G), MISSED LEFT (L), MISSED RIGHT (R)	# OF PUTTS / SCORE / PAR

OUT

1

2

3

4

5

6

7

8

9

SCORE

IN

10

11

12

13

14

15

16

17

18

BIRDIES _____	# GREENS IN	NOTES FOR NEXT PRACTICE SESSION: _____	**SCORE**
PARS _____	REGULATION _____	_____	
BOGEYS _____	# PUTTS _____	_____	
DOUBLE BOGEYS _____	# TEE SHOTS HIT_____	_____	**TOTAL SCORE**

PLAY

DATE _____

DAY _____

COURSE _____ RATING/SLOPE_____

	TEE SHOT-HIT FAIRWAY(F), OR MISSED LEFT (L), RIGHT (R)	GREEN IN REGULATION (G), MISSED LEFT (L), MISSED RIGHT (R)	# OF PUTTS / SCORE / PAR

OUT

1 _____

2 _____

3 _____

4 _____

5 _____

6 _____

7 _____

8 _____

9 _____

SCORE

IN

10 _____

11 _____

12 _____

13 _____

14 _____

15 _____

16 _____

17 _____

18 _____

BIRDIES _____	# GREENS IN	NOTES FOR NEXT PRACTICE SESSION: _____	**SCORE**
PARS _____	REGULATION _____	_____	
BOGEYS _____	# PUTTS _____	_____	
DOUBLE BOGEYS _____	# TEE SHOTS HIT_____	_____	**TOTAL SCORE**

"If you are caught on a golf course during a storm and are afraid of lightning, hold up a 1-iron. Not even God can hit a 1-iron."

-Lee Trevino

"The difference between golf and government is that in golf you can't improve your lie."

-George Deukmejian, former California Governor

PRACTICE

DATE _____

DAY _____

LOCATION _____

	DRILLS/NOTES	TARGET % HIT(H), LEFT(L), RIGHT(R)	AVG DISTANCE

SHORT IRONS
W _____

9 _____

8 _____

MIDDLE IRONS
7 _____

6 _____

5 _____

LONG IRONS
4 _____

3 _____

2 _____

WOODS
5 _____

4 _____

3 _____

1 _____

SPECIAL _____

CHECK LIST   ## PRACTICE FOCUS/NOTES

☐ TEMPO

☐ WEIGHT SHIFT

☐ BODY TURN

PRACTICE

DATE _____

DAY _____

LOCATION _____

	DRILLS/NOTES	TARGET % HIT(H), LEFT(L), RIGHT(R)	AVG DISTANCE

SHORT IRONS
W

9

8

MIDDLE IRONS
7

6

5

LONG IRONS
4

3

2

WOODS
5

4

3

1

SPECIAL

CHECK LIST   PRACTICE FOCUS/NOTES

☐ TEMPO

☐ WEIGHT SHIFT

☐ BODY TURN

PRACTICE

DATE _____
DAY _____

LOCATION _____

	DRILLS/NOTES	TARGET % HIT(H), LEFT(L), RIGHT(R)	AVG DISTANCE

SHORT IRONS

W

9

8

MIDDLE IRONS

7

6

5

LONG IRONS

4

3

2

WOODS

5

4

3

1

SPECIAL

CHECK LIST   **PRACTICE FOCUS/NOTES**

☐ TEMPO

☐ WEIGHT SHIFT

☐ BODY TURN

PRACTICE

DATE _____
DAY _____

LOCATION _____

	DRILLS/NOTES	TARGET % HIT(H), LEFT(L), RIGHT(R)	AVG DISTANCE

SHORT IRONS
W
9
8

MIDDLE IRONS
7
6
5

LONG IRONS
4
3
2

WOODS
5
4
3
1

SPECIAL

CHECK LIST   ## **PRACTICE FOCUS/NOTES**

☐ TEMPO

☐ WEIGHT SHIFT

☐ BODY TURN

PRACTICE

DATE _____
DAY _____

LOCATION _____

	DRILLS/NOTES	TARGET % HIT(H), LEFT(L), RIGHT(R)	AVG DISTANCE

SHORT IRONS
W

9

8

MIDDLE IRONS
7

6

5

LONG IRONS
4

3

2

WOODS
5

4

3

1

SPECIAL

CHECK LIST   PRACTICE FOCUS/NOTES

☐ TEMPO

☐ WEIGHT SHIFT

☐ BODY TURN

PRACTICE

DATE _____

DAY _____

LOCATION _____

	DRILLS/NOTES	TARGET % HIT(H), LEFT(L), RIGHT(R)	AVG DISTANCE

SHORT IRONS
W

9

8

MIDDLE IRONS
7

6

5

LONG IRONS
4

3

2

WOODS
5

4

3

1

SPECIAL

CHECK LIST   **PRACTICE FOCUS/NOTES**

☐ TEMPO

☐ WEIGHT SHIFT

☐ BODY TURN

RACTICE

DATE _____

DAY _____

LOCATION _____

	DRILLS/NOTES	TARGET % HIT(H), LEFT(L), RIGHT(R)	AVG DISTANCE

SHORT IRONS

W _____

9 _____

8 _____

MIDDLE IRONS

7 _____

6 _____

5 _____

LONG IRONS

4 _____

3 _____

2 _____

WOODS

5 _____

4 _____

3 _____

1 _____

SPECIAL _____

CHECK LIST   **PRACTICE FOCUS/NOTES**

☐ TEMPO

☐ WEIGHT SHIFT

☐ BODY TURN

PRACTICE

DATE _____

DAY _____

LOCATION _____

	DRILLS/NOTES	TARGET % HIT(H), LEFT(L), RIGHT(R)	AVG DISTANCE

SHORT IRONS
W _____

9 _____

8 _____

MIDDLE IRONS
7 _____

6 _____

5 _____

LONG IRONS
4 _____

3 _____

2 _____

WOODS
5 _____

4 _____

3 _____

1 _____

SPECIAL _____

CHECK LIST   ## **PRACTICE FOCUS/NOTES**

☐ TEMPO

☐ WEIGHT SHIFT

☐ BODY TURN

**P**RACTICE

DATE _____
DAY _____

LOCATION _____

	DRILLS/NOTES	TARGET % HIT(H), LEFT(L), RIGHT(R)	AVG DISTANCE

SHORT IRONS
W

9

8

MIDDLE IRONS
7

6

5

LONG IRONS
4

3

2

WOODS
5

4

3

1

SPECIAL

CHECK LIST

☐ TEMPO

☐ WEIGHT SHIFT

☐ BODY TURN

PRACTICE FOCUS/NOTES

PRACTICE

DATE _____
DAY _____

LOCATION _____

	DRILLS/NOTES	TARGET % HIT(H), LEFT(L), RIGHT(R)	AVG DISTANCE

SHORT IRONS
W _____

9 _____

8 _____

MIDDLE IRONS
7 _____

6 _____

5 _____

LONG IRONS
4 _____

3 _____

2 _____

WOODS
5 _____

4 _____

3 _____

1 _____

SPECIAL _____

CHECK LIST

☐ TEMPO

☐ WEIGHT SHIFT

☐ BODY TURN

PRACTICE FOCUS/NOTES
_____
_____
_____
_____
_____
_____

PRACTICE

DATE _____

DAY _____

LOCATION _____

	DRILLS/NOTES	TARGET % HIT(H), LEFT(L), RIGHT(R)	AVG DISTANCE

SHORT IRONS
W

9

8

MIDDLE IRONS
7

6

5

LONG IRONS
4

3

2

WOODS
5

4

3

1

SPECIAL

CHECK LIST

☐ TEMPO

☐ WEIGHT SHIFT

☐ BODY TURN

PRACTICE FOCUS/NOTES

PRACTICE

DATE _____

DAY _____

LOCATION _____

	DRILLS/NOTES	TARGET % HIT(H), LEFT(L), RIGHT(R)	AVG DISTANCE

SHORT IRONS

W

9

8

MIDDLE IRONS

7

6

5

LONG IRONS

4

3

2

WOODS

5

4

3

1

SPECIAL

CHECK LIST   PRACTICE FOCUS/NOTES

☐ TEMPO

☐ WEIGHT SHIFT

☐ BODY TURN

RACTICE

DATE _____
DAY _____

LOCATION _____

| | DRILLS/NOTES | TARGET %
HIT(H), LEFT(L), RIGHT(R) | AVG DISTANCE |

SHORT IRONS
W _____

9 _____

8 _____

MIDDLE IRONS
7 _____

6 _____

5 _____

LONG IRONS
4 _____

3 _____

2 _____

WOODS
5 _____

4 _____

3 _____

1 _____

SPECIAL _____

CHECK LIST   PRACTICE FOCUS/NOTES

☐ TEMPO

☐ WEIGHT SHIFT

☐ BODY TURN

RACTICE

DATE _____
DAY _____

LOCATION _____

	DRILLS/NOTES	TARGET % HIT(H), LEFT(L), RIGHT(R)	AVG DISTANCE

SHORT IRONS

W _____

9 _____

8 _____

MIDDLE IRONS

7 _____

6 _____

5 _____

LONG IRONS

4 _____

3 _____

2 _____

WOODS

5 _____

4 _____

3 _____

1 _____

SPECIAL _____

CHECK LIST   PRACTICE FOCUS/NOTES

☐ TEMPO

☐ WEIGHT SHIFT

☐ BODY TURN

"A sick appendix is not as difficult to deal
with as a five-foot putt."

-Gene Sarazen

*"If you watch a game, it's fun.
If you play it, it's recreation.
If you work at it, it's golf."*

-Bob Hope

RACTICE

DATE _____
DAY _____

LOCATION _____

| | DRILLS/NOTES | TARGET %
HIT(H), LEFT(L), RIGHT(R) | AVG DISTANCE |

SHORT IRONS

W _____

9 _____

8 _____

MIDDLE IRONS

7 _____

6 _____

5 _____

LONG IRONS

4 _____

3 _____

2 _____

WOODS

5 _____

4 _____

3 _____

1 _____

SPECIAL _____

CHECK LIST   PRACTICE FOCUS/NOTES

☐ TEMPO _____

☐ WEIGHT SHIFT _____

☐ BODY TURN _____

RACTICE

LOCATION _____

	DRILLS/NOTES	TARGET % HIT(H), LEFT(L), RIGHT(R)	AVG DISTANCE

SHORT IRONS

W

9

8

MIDDLE IRONS

7

6

5

LONG IRONS

4

3

2

WOODS

5

4

3

1

SPECIAL

CHECK LIST   ## PRACTICE FOCUS/NOTES

☐ TEMPO

☐ WEIGHT SHIFT

☐ BODY TURN

PRACTICE

DATE _____
DAY _____

LOCATION _____

	DRILLS/NOTES	TARGET % HIT(H), LEFT(L), RIGHT(R)	AVG DISTANCE

SHORT IRONS

W _____

9 _____

8 _____

MIDDLE IRONS

7 _____

6 _____

5 _____

LONG IRONS

4 _____

3 _____

2 _____

WOODS

5 _____

4 _____

3 _____

1 _____

SPECIAL _____

CHECK LIST   PRACTICE FOCUS/NOTES

☐ TEMPO

☐ WEIGHT SHIFT

☐ BODY TURN

PRACTICE

DATE _____

DAY _____

LOCATION _____

	DRILLS/NOTES	TARGET % HIT(H), LEFT(L), RIGHT(R)	AVG DISTANCE

SHORT IRONS

W _____

9 _____

8 _____

MIDDLE IRONS

7 _____

6 _____

5 _____

LONG IRONS

4 _____

3 _____

2 _____

WOODS

5 _____

4 _____

3 _____

1 _____

SPECIAL _____

CHECK LIST

☐ TEMPO

☐ WEIGHT SHIFT

☐ BODY TURN

PRACTICE FOCUS/NOTES

_____
_____
_____
_____
_____
_____

RACTICE

DATE _____

DAY _____

LOCATION _____

	DRILLS/NOTES	TARGET % HIT(H), LEFT(L), RIGHT(R)	AVG DISTANCE

SHORT IRONS
W _____

9 _____

8 _____

MIDDLE IRONS
7 _____

6 _____

5 _____

LONG IRONS
4 _____

3 _____

2 _____

WOODS
5 _____

4 _____

3 _____

1 _____

SPECIAL _____

CHECK LIST   PRACTICE FOCUS/NOTES

☐ TEMPO   _____

☐ WEIGHT SHIFT   _____

☐ BODY TURN   _____

_____

_____

PRACTICE

DATE _____
DAY _____

LOCATION _____

	DRILLS/NOTES	TARGET % HIT(H), LEFT(L), RIGHT(R)	AVG DISTANCE

SHORT IRONS
W _____

9 _____

8 _____

MIDDLE IRONS
7 _____

6 _____

5 _____

LONG IRONS
4 _____

3 _____

2 _____

WOODS
5 _____

4 _____

3 _____

1 _____

SPECIAL _____

CHECK LIST   PRACTICE FOCUS/NOTES

☐ TEMPO

☐ WEIGHT SHIFT

☐ BODY TURN

RACTICE

DATE _____

DAY _____

LOCATION _____

	DRILLS/NOTES	TARGET % HIT(H), LEFT(L), RIGHT(R)	AVG DISTANCE

SHORT IRONS
W

9

8

MIDDLE IRONS
7

6

5

LONG IRONS
4

3

2

WOODS
5

4

3

1

SPECIAL

CHECK LIST   PRACTICE FOCUS/NOTES

☐ TEMPO

☐ WEIGHT SHIFT

☐ BODY TURN

PRACTICE

DATE _____
DAY _____

LOCATION _____

	DRILLS/NOTES	TARGET % HIT(H), LEFT(L), RIGHT(R)	AVG DISTANCE

SHORT IRONS

W _____

9 _____

8 _____

MIDDLE IRONS

7 _____

6 _____

5 _____

LONG IRONS

4 _____

3 _____

2 _____

WOODS

5 _____

4 _____

3 _____

1 _____

SPECIAL _____

CHECK LIST PRACTICE FOCUS/NOTES

☐ TEMPO

☐ WEIGHT SHIFT

☐ BODY TURN

PRACTICE

DATE _____

DAY _____

LOCATION _____

	DRILLS/NOTES	TARGET % HIT(H), LEFT(L), RIGHT(R)	AVG DISTANCE

SHORT IRONS
W _____

9 _____

8 _____

MIDDLE IRONS
7 _____

6 _____

5 _____

LONG IRONS
4 _____

3 _____

2 _____

WOODS
5 _____

4 _____

3 _____

1 _____

SPECIAL _____

CHECK LIST   PRACTICE FOCUS/NOTES

☐ TEMPO

☐ WEIGHT SHIFT

☐ BODY TURN

RACTICE

DATE _____
DAY _____

LOCATION _____

	DRILLS/NOTES	TARGET % HIT(H), LEFT(L), RIGHT(R)	AVG DISTANCE

SHORT IRONS

W _____

9 _____

8 _____

MIDDLE IRONS

7 _____

6 _____

5 _____

LONG IRONS

4 _____

3 _____

2 _____

WOODS

5 _____

4 _____

3 _____

1 _____

SPECIAL _____

CHECK LIST ## PRACTICE FOCUS/NOTES

☐ TEMPO

☐ WEIGHT SHIFT

☐ BODY TURN

PRACTICE

DATE _____

DAY _____

LOCATION _____

	DRILLS/NOTES	TARGET % HIT(H), LEFT(L), RIGHT(R)	AVG DISTANCE

SHORT IRONS
W _____

9 _____

8 _____

MIDDLE IRONS
7 _____

6 _____

5 _____

LONG IRONS
4 _____

3 _____

2 _____

WOODS
5 _____

4 _____

3 _____

1 _____

SPECIAL _____

CHECK LIST   PRACTICE FOCUS/NOTES

☐ TEMPO

☐ WEIGHT SHIFT

☐ BODY TURN

RACTICE

DATE _____

DAY _____

LOCATION _____

	DRILLS/NOTES	TARGET % HIT(H), LEFT(L), RIGHT(R)	AVG DISTANCE

SHORT IRONS

W _____

9 _____

8 _____

MIDDLE IRONS

7 _____

6 _____

5 _____

LONG IRONS

4 _____

3 _____

2 _____

WOODS

5 _____

4 _____

3 _____

1 _____

SPECIAL _____

CHECK LIST   PRACTICE FOCUS/NOTES

☐ TEMPO

☐ WEIGHT SHIFT

☐ BODY TURN

RACTICE

DATE _____

DAY _____

LOCATION _____

	DRILLS/NOTES	TARGET % HIT(H), LEFT(L), RIGHT(R)	AVG DISTANCE

SHORT IRONS
W _____

9 _____

8 _____

MIDDLE IRONS
7 _____

6 _____

5 _____

LONG IRONS
4 _____

3 _____

2 _____

WOODS
5 _____

4 _____

3 _____

1 _____

SPECIAL _____

CHECK LIST

PRACTICE FOCUS/NOTES

☐ TEMPO

☐ WEIGHT SHIFT

☐ BODY TURN

RACTICE

DATE _____

DAY _____

LOCATION _____

	DRILLS/NOTES	TARGET % HIT(H), LEFT(L), RIGHT(R)	AVG DISTANCE

SHORT IRONS
W _____

9 _____

8 _____

MIDDLE IRONS
7 _____

6 _____

5 _____

LONG IRONS
4 _____

3 _____

2 _____

WOODS
5 _____

4 _____

3 _____

1 _____

SPECIAL _____

CHECK LIST   PRACTICE FOCUS/NOTES

☐ TEMPO

☐ WEIGHT SHIFT

☐ BODY TURN

"Golf and sex are about the only things you can enjoy without being good at."

-Jimmy Demaret

*"Golf: a game in which
you claim the privileges of age,
and retain the playthings of childhood."*

-Samuel Johnson

RACTICE

DATE _____

DAY _____

LOCATION _____

	DRILLS/NOTES	TARGET % HIT(H), LEFT(L), RIGHT(R)	AVG DISTANCE

SHORT IRONS
W

9

8

MIDDLE IRONS
7

6

5

LONG IRONS
4

3

2

WOODS
5

4

3

1

SPECIAL

CHECK LIST

☐ TEMPO

☐ WEIGHT SHIFT

☐ BODY TURN

PRACTICE FOCUS/NOTES

PRACTICE

DATE _____
DAY _____

LOCATION _____

	DRILLS/NOTES	TARGET % HIT(H), LEFT(L), RIGHT(R)	AVG DISTANCE

SHORT IRONS
W _____

9 _____

8 _____

MIDDLE IRONS
7 _____

6 _____

5 _____

LONG IRONS
4 _____

3 _____

2 _____

WOODS
5 _____

4 _____

3 _____

1 _____

SPECIAL _____

CHECK LIST

☐ TEMPO

☐ WEIGHT SHIFT

☐ BODY TURN

PRACTICE FOCUS/NOTES

_____
_____
_____
_____
_____
_____

PRACTICE

DATE _____

DAY _____

LOCATION _____

	DRILLS/NOTES	TARGET % HIT(H), LEFT(L), RIGHT(R)	AVG DISTANCE

SHORT IRONS
W

9

8

MIDDLE IRONS
7

6

5

LONG IRONS
4

3

2

WOODS
5

4

3

1

SPECIAL

CHECK LIST

☐ TEMPO

☐ WEIGHT SHIFT

☐ BODY TURN

PRACTICE FOCUS/NOTES

_____
_____
_____
_____
_____
_____
_____

PRACTICE

DATE _____

DAY _____

LOCATION _____

	DRILLS/NOTES	TARGET % HIT(H), LEFT(L), RIGHT(R)	AVG DISTANCE

SHORT IRONS

W _____

9 _____

8 _____

MIDDLE IRONS

7 _____

6 _____

5 _____

LONG IRONS

4 _____

3 _____

2 _____

WOODS

5 _____

4 _____

3 _____

1 _____

SPECIAL _____

CHECK LIST   PRACTICE FOCUS/NOTES

☐ TEMPO

☐ WEIGHT SHIFT

☐ BODY TURN

**P**RACTICE

DATE _____

DAY _____

LOCATION _____

	DRILLS/NOTES	TARGET % HIT(H), LEFT(L), RIGHT(R)	AVG DISTANCE

SHORT IRONS

W

9

8

MIDDLE IRONS

7

6

5

LONG IRONS

4

3

2

WOODS

5

4

3

1

SPECIAL

CHECK LIST

☐ TEMPO

☐ WEIGHT SHIFT

☐ BODY TURN

PRACTICE FOCUS/NOTES

RACTICE

DATE _____
DAY _____

LOCATION _____

	DRILLS/NOTES	TARGET % HIT(H), LEFT(L), RIGHT(R)	AVG DISTANCE

SHORT IRONS

W _____

9 _____

8 _____

MIDDLE IRONS

7 _____

6 _____

5 _____

LONG IRONS

4 _____

3 _____

2 _____

WOODS

5 _____

4 _____

3 _____

1 _____

SPECIAL _____

CHECK LIST   PRACTICE FOCUS/NOTES

☐ TEMPO

☐ WEIGHT SHIFT

☐ BODY TURN

PRACTICE

DATE _____
DAY _____

LOCATION _____

| | DRILLS/NOTES | TARGET % HIT(H), LEFT(L), RIGHT(R) | AVG DISTANCE |

SHORT IRONS
W _____

9 _____

8 _____

MIDDLE IRONS
7 _____

6 _____

5 _____

LONG IRONS
4 _____

3 _____

2 _____

WOODS
5 _____

4 _____

3 _____

1 _____

SPECIAL _____

CHECK LIST   **PRACTICE FOCUS/NOTES**

☐ TEMPO

☐ WEIGHT SHIFT

☐ BODY TURN

RACTICE

DATE _____

DAY _____

LOCATION _____

	DRILLS/NOTES	TARGET % HIT(H), LEFT(L), RIGHT(R)	AVG DISTANCE

SHORT IRONS
W _____

9 _____

8 _____

MIDDLE IRONS
7 _____

6 _____

5 _____

LONG IRONS
4 _____

3 _____

2 _____

WOODS
5 _____

4 _____

3 _____

1 _____

SPECIAL _____

CHECK LIST   PRACTICE FOCUS/NOTES

☐ TEMPO   _____

☐ WEIGHT SHIFT   _____

☐ BODY TURN   _____

RACTICE

DATE _____

DAY _____

LOCATION _____

	DRILLS/NOTES	TARGET % HIT(H), LEFT(L), RIGHT(R)	AVG DISTANCE

SHORT IRONS
W _____

9 _____

8 _____

MIDDLE IRONS
7 _____

6 _____

5 _____

LONG IRONS
4 _____

3 _____

2 _____

WOODS
5 _____

4 _____

3 _____

1 _____

SPECIAL _____

CHECK LIST   PRACTICE FOCUS/NOTES

☐ TEMPO

☐ WEIGHT SHIFT

☐ BODY TURN

PRACTICE

DATE _____

DAY _____

LOCATION _____

	DRILLS/NOTES	TARGET % HIT(H), LEFT(L), RIGHT(R)	AVG DISTANCE

SHORT IRONS

W _____

9 _____

8 _____

MIDDLE IRONS

7 _____

6 _____

5 _____

LONG IRONS

4 _____

3 _____

2 _____

WOODS

5 _____

4 _____

3 _____

1 _____

SPECIAL _____

CHECK LIST   PRACTICE FOCUS/NOTES

☐ TEMPO

☐ WEIGHT SHIFT

☐ BODY TURN

PRACTICE

DATE _____

DAY _____

LOCATION _____

	DRILLS/NOTES	TARGET % HIT(H), LEFT(L), RIGHT(R)	AVG DISTANCE

SHORT IRONS

W _____

9 _____

8 _____

MIDDLE IRONS

7 _____

6 _____

5 _____

LONG IRONS

4 _____

3 _____

2 _____

WOODS

5 _____

4 _____

3 _____

1 _____

SPECIAL _____

CHECK LIST   PRACTICE FOCUS/NOTES

☐ TEMPO

☐ WEIGHT SHIFT

☐ BODY TURN

PRACTICE

DATE _____
DAY _____

LOCATION _____

	DRILLS/NOTES	TARGET % HIT(H), LEFT(L), RIGHT(R)	AVG DISTANCE

SHORT IRONS

W _____

9 _____

8 _____

MIDDLE IRONS

7 _____

6 _____

5 _____

LONG IRONS

4 _____

3 _____

2 _____

WOODS

5 _____

4 _____

3 _____

1 _____

SPECIAL _____

CHECK LIST   PRACTICE FOCUS/NOTES

☐ TEMPO

☐ WEIGHT SHIFT

☐ BODY TURN

RACTICE

DATE _____

DAY _____

LOCATION _____

	DRILLS/NOTES	TARGET % HIT(H), LEFT(L), RIGHT(R)	AVG DISTANCE

SHORT IRONS

W _____

9 _____

8 _____

MIDDLE IRONS

7 _____

6 _____

5 _____

LONG IRONS

4 _____

3 _____

2 _____

WOODS

5 _____

4 _____

3 _____

1 _____

SPECIAL _____

CHECK LIST   PRACTICE FOCUS/NOTES

☐ TEMPO

☐ WEIGHT SHIFT

☐ BODY TURN

PRACTICE

DATE _____
DAY _____

LOCATION _____

	DRILLS/NOTES	TARGET % HIT(H), LEFT(L), RIGHT(R)	AVG DISTANCE

SHORT IRONS
W _____

9 _____

8 _____

MIDDLE IRONS
7 _____

6 _____

5 _____

LONG IRONS
4 _____

3 _____

2 _____

WOODS
5 _____

4 _____

3 _____

1 _____

SPECIAL _____

CHECK LIST

☐ TEMPO

☐ WEIGHT SHIFT

☐ BODY TURN

PRACTICE FOCUS/NOTES

_____
_____
_____
_____
_____
_____

"Golf is the most fun you can have without taking your clothes off."

-Chi Chi Rodriguez

"The gods too are fond of a joke."

-Aristotle

PRACTICE

DATE _____
DAY _____

LOCATION _____

	DRILLS/NOTES	TARGET % HIT(H), LEFT(L), RIGHT(R)	AVG DISTANCE

SHORT IRONS

W _____

9 _____

8 _____

MIDDLE IRONS

7 _____

6 _____

5 _____

LONG IRONS

4 _____

3 _____

2 _____

WOODS

5 _____

4 _____

3 _____

1 _____

SPECIAL _____

CHECK LIST   **PRACTICE FOCUS/NOTES**

☐ TEMPO

☐ WEIGHT SHIFT

☐ BODY TURN

PRACTICE

DATE _____

DAY _____

LOCATION _____

	DRILLS/NOTES	TARGET % HIT(H), LEFT(L), RIGHT(R)	AVG DISTANCE

SHORT IRONS

W

9

8

MIDDLE IRONS

7

6

5

LONG IRONS

4

3

2

WOODS

5

4

3

1

SPECIAL

CHECK LIST

☐ TEMPO

☐ WEIGHT SHIFT

☐ BODY TURN

PRACTICE FOCUS/NOTES

RACTICE

DATE _____
DAY _____

LOCATION _____

	DRILLS/NOTES	TARGET % HIT(H), LEFT(L), RIGHT(R)	AVG DISTANCE

SHORT IRONS
W _____

9 _____

8 _____

MIDDLE IRONS
7 _____

6 _____

5 _____

LONG IRONS
4 _____

3 _____

2 _____

WOODS
5 _____

4 _____

3 _____

1 _____

SPECIAL _____

CHECK LIST   PRACTICE FOCUS/NOTES

☐ TEMPO

☐ WEIGHT SHIFT

☐ BODY TURN

RACTICE

DATE _____

DAY _____

LOCATION _____

	DRILLS/NOTES	TARGET % HIT(H), LEFT(L), RIGHT(R)	AVG DISTANCE

SHORT IRONS
W

9

8

MIDDLE IRONS
7

6

5

LONG IRONS
4

3

2

WOODS
5

4

3

1

SPECIAL

CHECK LIST   PRACTICE FOCUS/NOTES

☐ TEMPO

☐ WEIGHT SHIFT

☐ BODY TURN

RACTICE

DATE _____

DAY _____

LOCATION _____

	DRILLS/NOTES	TARGET % HIT(H), LEFT(L), RIGHT(R)	AVG DISTANCE

SHORT IRONS
W

9

8

MIDDLE IRONS
7

6

5

LONG IRONS
4

3

2

WOODS
5

4

3

1

SPECIAL

CHECK LIST   PRACTICE FOCUS/NOTES

☐ TEMPO

☐ WEIGHT SHIFT

☐ BODY TURN

**P**RACTICE

DATE _____
DAY _____

LOCATION _____

| | DRILLS/NOTES | TARGET %
HIT(H), LEFT(L), RIGHT(R) | AVG DISTANCE |

SHORT IRONS

W _____

9 _____

8 _____

MIDDLE IRONS

7 _____

6 _____

5 _____

LONG IRONS

4 _____

3 _____

2 _____

WOODS

5 _____

4 _____

3 _____

1 _____

SPECIAL _____

CHECK LIST   PRACTICE FOCUS/NOTES

☐ TEMPO

☐ WEIGHT SHIFT

☐ BODY TURN

RACTICE

DATE _____
DAY _____

LOCATION _____

	DRILLS/NOTES	TARGET % HIT(H), LEFT(L), RIGHT(R)	AVG DISTANCE

SHORT IRONS

W _____

9 _____

8 _____

MIDDLE IRONS

7 _____

6 _____

5 _____

LONG IRONS

4 _____

3 _____

2 _____

WOODS

5 _____

4 _____

3 _____

1 _____

SPECIAL _____

CHECK LIST   **PRACTICE FOCUS/NOTES**

☐ TEMPO

☐ WEIGHT SHIFT

☐ BODY TURN

PRACTICE

DATE _____

DAY _____

LOCATION _____

	DRILLS/NOTES	TARGET % HIT(H), LEFT(L), RIGHT(R)	AVG DISTANCE

SHORT IRONS
W _____

9 _____

8 _____

MIDDLE IRONS
7 _____

6 _____

5 _____

LONG IRONS
4 _____

3 _____

2 _____

WOODS
5 _____

4 _____

3 _____

1 _____

SPECIAL _____

CHECK LIST   PRACTICE FOCUS/NOTES

☐ TEMPO

☐ WEIGHT SHIFT

☐ BODY TURN

PRACTICE

DATE _____

DAY _____

LOCATION _____

	DRILLS/NOTES	TARGET % HIT(H), LEFT(L), RIGHT(R)	AVG DISTANCE

SHORT IRONS

W _____

9 _____

8 _____

MIDDLE IRONS

7 _____

6 _____

5 _____

LONG IRONS

4 _____

3 _____

2 _____

WOODS

5 _____

4 _____

3 _____

1 _____

SPECIAL _____

CHECK LIST   **PRACTICE FOCUS/NOTES**

☐ TEMPO

☐ WEIGHT SHIFT

☐ BODY TURN

PRACTICE

DATE _____
DAY _____

LOCATION _____

	DRILLS/NOTES	TARGET % HIT(H), LEFT(L), RIGHT(R)	AVG DISTANCE

SHORT IRONS
W _____

9 _____

8 _____

MIDDLE IRONS
7 _____

6 _____

5 _____

LONG IRONS
4 _____

3 _____

2 _____

WOODS
5 _____

4 _____

3 _____

1 _____

SPECIAL _____

CHECK LIST   ## PRACTICE FOCUS/NOTES

☐ TEMPO

☐ WEIGHT SHIFT

☐ BODY TURN

RACTICE

DATE _____

DAY _____

LOCATION _____

	DRILLS/NOTES	TARGET % HIT(H), LEFT(L), RIGHT(R)	AVG DISTANCE

SHORT IRONS

W _____

9 _____

8 _____

MIDDLE IRONS

7 _____

6 _____

5 _____

LONG IRONS

4 _____

3 _____

2 _____

WOODS

5 _____

4 _____

3 _____

1 _____

SPECIAL _____

CHECK LIST   PRACTICE FOCUS/NOTES

☐ TEMPO

☐ WEIGHT SHIFT

☐ BODY TURN

RACTICE

LOCATION _____

	DRILLS/NOTES	TARGET % HIT(H), LEFT(L), RIGHT(R)	AVG DISTANCE

SHORT IRONS

W _____

9 _____

8 _____

MIDDLE IRONS

7 _____

6 _____

5 _____

LONG IRONS

4 _____

3 _____

2 _____

WOODS

5 _____

4 _____

3 _____

1 _____

SPECIAL _____

CHECK LIST   PRACTICE FOCUS/NOTES

☐ TEMPO

☐ WEIGHT SHIFT

☐ BODY TURN

PRACTICE

DATE _____

DAY _____

LOCATION _____

	DRILLS/NOTES	TARGET % HIT(H), LEFT(L), RIGHT(R)	AVG DISTANCE

SHORT IRONS
W

9

8

MIDDLE IRONS
7

6

5

LONG IRONS
4

3

2

WOODS
5

4

3

1

SPECIAL

CHECK LIST

PRACTICE FOCUS/NOTES

☐ TEMPO

☐ WEIGHT SHIFT

☐ BODY TURN

RACTICE

LOCATION _____

	DRILLS/NOTES	TARGET % HIT(H), LEFT(L), RIGHT(R)	AVG DISTANCE

SHORT IRONS

W _____

9 _____

8 _____

MIDDLE IRONS

7 _____

6 _____

5 _____

LONG IRONS

4 _____

3 _____

2 _____

WOODS

5 _____

4 _____

3 _____

1 _____

SPECIAL _____

CHECK LIST   ## PRACTICE FOCUS/NOTES

☐ TEMPO

☐ WEIGHT SHIFT

☐ BODY TURN

"If a lot of people gripped a knife and fork like they do a golf club, they'd starve to death."

-Sam Snead